TENNIS MADE EASY

count ONE!
to top
tennis
technique

by JOEL BRECHEEN

1978 EDITION

W

Published by
Melvin Powers
WILSHIRE BOOK COMPANY
12015 Sherman Road
No. Hollywood, California 91605
Telephone: (213) 875-1711

About the Author ...

JOEL BRECHEEN began playing tennis when he was 10 years old, and once he started he has never stopped. Neither the Depression nor World War II managed to diminish his eagerness or joy in the game. Much of his youth was spent in California, where he was a constant figure around the courts, watching the top players, both amateur and pro, and learning the finer points of the game from his observations, and from his always trying to get a game with someone who was a better player than he was.

He plays tennis whenever he can find a partner and a court. While serving with Army Intelligence, he found old courts in Burma to play on; and built a court in mountainous west China, using gasoline drums for backstops.

Turning pro in 1952, he developed and built his own tennis club in Phoenix. He has also been the pro at the Town and Country Club, St. Paul, Minnesota, at such Phoenix resorts as Paradise, Royal Palms, and Jokake Inns, and at Skyline Country Club in Tucson. Throughout these years, he has concentrated on working with youngsters, and many of his pupils, including his two daughters, have been winners of various state and regional tournaments.

A man of diverse interests and skills, Brecheen is an avid chess player, has owned and operated a guest ranch (where he had a standing offer of free room and board to anyone who could beat him at both tennis *and* chess), holds a master's degree in education, reads and writes poetry, has taught creative writing, and is an accomplished builder.

Brecheen and his Phoenix tennis club were featured in *Life* magazine in 1958. More recently, he has lived with his family on a small ranch in southeastern Arizona, managing to combine teaching high school English with coaching high school and college tennis teams, as well as individuals. He still competes regularly in tournaments.

Copyright © 1969
Palo Verde Publishing Co., Inc.
P.O. Box 5783
Tucson, Arizona 85703
All Rights Reserved
Manufactured in the U.S.A.

Photography by TED OFFRET

L.C. Catalog Card No. 70-95603

ISBN 0-87980-160-3

Foreword

TENNIS, OF ALL THE GAMES WE PLAY, probably provides the best combination of pure enjoyment and health-promoting exercise. Its participants come from all age groups, from the youngster on a city tennis court to a king of Sweden in his eighties.

The alarming death rate from vascular disease (heart attacks, high blood pressure, and strokes), which often strikes people in their prime, has already reached epidemic proportions in the United States and other countries of the Western world. Basically, these heart attacks and strokes are the end result of the deterioration of the blood vessels in the heart, brain, and other parts of the body.

One logically asks, "What causes the trouble in these blood vessels? How can it be prevented?" Scientists all over the world are working on the problem. While the answers are not all in, some clues stand out: overwhelming evidence suggests that the three factors of *heredity, diet,* and *exercise* are vital. One cannot choose his parents, and thus his heredity, but the other two factors are within our power to alter and manipulate, so that life can probably be made healthier, longer, and more enjoyable.

A preponderance of research incriminates cholesterol as one of the major contributors to the degenerative processes in the blood vessels. This cholesterol is most concentrated in saturated fats. Thus, *diet* is a factor that is in the power of the individual to control.

When it comes to *exercise,* the third factor in blood vessel disease, a tremendous amount of evidence is accumulating to show that regular, daily, strenuous exercise is very definitely conducive to a healthier and longer life. The earlier in life exercise is begun the better, but science has discovered that, contrary to former ideas, vigorous exercise may be initiated at almost any age, even by those not used to it, provided one works up to it in graduated steps.

Thus, we come to the actual intent of this Foreword — to praise tennis and the author of this book. I had long been aware of the value of exercise and bought numerous gadgets to entice myself into exercising regularly. But after an initial spurt of enthusiasm with each, the exercise afforded me no real pleasure, and the gadget was eventually consigned to a dusty corner.

Finally, a friend suggested tennis. Now, to a man past his youth this sounded intriguing, but I wondered if I was too old to begin the game. Being a man who rides each hobby hard, however, I decided to build a court of my own and learn to play. As my ability increased, I found better partners, worked on my strokes, and the more I improved the more fun I had and the better I felt.

An excellent book, *How to Keep Fit and Enjoy It,* by Dr. Warren R. Guild of Harvard Medical School, emphasizes the value of *enjoying* an exercise. For most people, exercise has to be pleasurable to provide an enduring interest, and I know of no mechanical device that can meet this test. Exercise should be fun, play.

In a consideration of all possible games, tennis stands out as the one which affords the most pleasure and exercise to people of all ages. It is enjoyable and relatively inexpensive. Tennis, especially singles — or even practice alone — necessitates a great deal of running, which is recognized as being the best single conditioner for heart and body.

At a recent international meeting for the study of heart disease and related conditions, it was unanimously agreed that everyone should be given the following prescription for health and longevity: "Avoid overeating, don't smoke, try to avoid stress situations, and exercise vigorously and steadily throughout your lifetime." To this I would add, "Make mine tennis!"

And now a most important word about author Joel Brecheen: After five years of intensive study and practice, I felt I had a modicum of insight into the game of tennis, augmented by lessons over the years from various professionals. *Nothing,* however, has ever improved my game as much as the intensive coaching given me by Mr. Brecheen during a vacation.

The method set forth in *Count One! To Top Tennis Technique* represents the distillation of Joel Brecheen's years of experience as a tennis professional, and provides expert advice and assistance for the beginner, for the player wishing to improve his game, and for the coach. I cannot recommend Brecheen's method highly enough.

Carl W. Stroud, M.D.

A Note from the Author

"I used to play tennis, but it's too rough now. You see, I'm almost forty years old." This explanation is usually delivered with a little regretful smile. All the active part of my life, which (thank heavens!) has been most of it, I have heard the above statement in one variation or another. Mostly, in past years, I put it down to sheer laziness. Had these people, I wondered, actually been brainwashed into believing that their bodies were not their own after the "witching age" of forty? After arguing heatedly with the first six hundred or so, I gave up, thereafter simply staring in grave disbelief and muttering to myself, "Fools! Fools!"

For the overconfident, life always has ready a rap on the knuckles. It made no exception for me. As the years passed, I came reluctantly and finally to the conclusion that most of these "lazy" fellows were not actually lazy. Their statement was correct, and my regarding them as "fools" was wrong. I apologize to all whom I have slandered. My reneging friends were correct.

The conclusion I came to — which, incidentally, is the reason for this book — is that if you do not play tennis *correctly,* it IS too tough, too much a strain on the isolated parts of the body.

What a fate, to be forced so early to separate yourself from this wonderful game, from this philosophy of fairness, this intensive effort which employs *all* your physical and mental capabilities to the point of absolute exhilaration! How tragic is this abandonment and exile because you simply did not know a METHOD of playing tennis that would let you play it with pleasure and benefit *all* your life!

Thus, my purpose herein is to describe a surefire METHOD by which the joy of the game of tennis can be learned and experienced at any age, extended for those who have been pursuing the sport, and guaranteed *lifelong* for the young who are just beginning. It is true. You need not become a premature exile from the pleasures of this most excellent of games.

The book begins with the basic concept of my approach. In later chapters, I outline technically the METHOD by which this concept can be brought physically into your possession. My authority is that of one who has played tennis most of his life (since age ten), and has given it during all this time the fullest measure of his thought and love.

Few books of this nature about tennis have appeared in print, and the explanation is not far to seek. Each teaching professional has his own method, his stock in trade. It is evolved from years of study, experiment, and trial and error, and bought with blood and sweat. His ways of imparting these secrets of leverage and skill constitute much of his personal treasure. Naturally, he will guard it!

Due to the nature of the game, tennis players, by and large, are resourceful and independent. The best of the teaching professionals are in the same category. Independently, then, I have decided, as the years roll on, that I would prefer to make my METHOD more widely known than is possible only by direct contact. I have been influenced, as well, by the pleas of my students to "put it down" so that they could refer to it later. Tennis coaches whom I have taught are the most vocal of the "put it in a book" group.

Last, but of primary importance, the METHOD has contributed to the development of many championship tennis players, and to the physical well-being of hundreds of other students. The tennis game of every one of them is marked, in varying degrees, with strokes of utility and beauty.

With this book is it my hope to partially repay this greatest of all games for what it has given to me. So, with a friendly wave of my hand to you prospective students, here is my METHOD.

JOEL BRECHEEN

Boot and Racquet Ranch

Table of Contents

How To Use This Book

This book is designed *equally* for the student — beginner or otherwise — and for the teacher, whether he is a coach, friend, parent, or relative.

But it is AIMED at the STUDENT. Countless years of teaching have made it impossible for me to write it in any other way. Throughout, I have tried to pretend that I am actually on the court with the student. If you are the teacher (coach, parent, or other), you are acting as my "stand-in" during each step of every lesson.

The "teacher" does NOT have to know how to play tennis for the student to learn how. As a matter of fact, there is no reason why two people, neither of whom knows how to play, cannot both "learn from scratch" to play a good game of tennis, following the instructions in this book. But because my *way* of teaching comprises an entire METHOD, what *is* important is that both student and the person acting as teacher read each chapter carefully, and follow the instructions faithfully.

My *method* does not mean that all who learn from me play exactly alike. Rather, my *method* teaches you how to execute each of the five tennis strokes in ONE COUNT, using your whole body rather than just your arm. WITHIN this *method,* each student develops his own style of play.

Regardless of whether the student is a raw beginner, has played a little tennis, or is a proficient player anxious to improve one or more of his strokes, and *regardless* of whether the teacher is a coach or does not play at all, both student and teacher MUST read each chapter carefully if my METHOD is to be understood, and maximum benefit derived from each lesson.

► ARRANGEMENT OF THE BOOK

The book has three sections: (1) A preliminary, but *extremely important* section containing three chapters, "Before You Begin," "Basic, Basic Points," and "Preparation for the First Lesson"; (2) the six lessons for the five strokes that comprise the game of tennis, and "The Game Itself"; (3) a final section consisting of chapters covering "Subtleties for the Advanced" and "Tips to the Coach."

In Section 2, each of the lessons for the five strokes is further divided into two parts: The *first part* gives a technical explanation of the stroke and detailed instructions for learning it. This part is ALWAYS MARKED BY A TENNIS RACQUET AT THE BEGINNING AND THE END. The *second part* tells you the best ways of practicing with a partner or by yourself, and reminds you of things to remember about the stroke.

► IF YOU ARE A BEGINNER OR HAVE PLAYED ONLY A LITTLE

Even before setting foot on a court, both you and your teacher MUST read the three chapters in Section 1, if my METHOD is to be understood. You should prepare your hand and racquet as explained in "Preparation for the First Lesson."

Now, you're ready for the first actual lesson — the Forehand Stroke.

TAKE THE BOOK TO THE COURT WITH YOU. Ideally, the "coach" or "teacher" should read aloud and the student should listen, and then carry out the lesson instructions. Open the book to "The Forehand Stroke." Now both you and your teacher must read the material that is marked off by tennis racquets, and the two of you should discuss what is expected of each of you.

Then, begin the lesson, following each portion of it EXACTLY as I have explained it. (Bear in mind that the book is *written* to the *student*.) Do NOT jump over any sections. But also, do not be discouraged if it takes you a little longer in some instances than I have indicated. If the teacher is having trouble tossing the balls just where they should go, do not despair. This *can* take a little practice (even if the teacher is a coach), but it will soon become easy.

If both the student and "teacher" are beginners and both wish to learn:

> The first student should stay with the lesson long enough to make some real progress in hitting the ball as instructed. Then, if time permits and you're both not too tired from the unaccustomed exercise, trade places. If you're both tired, wait until next time to trade places.

IMPORTANT! Acquire *basic mastery* of the Forehand Stroke before proceeding to the next lesson. Do not try to rush through this book in just a few sessions at the court. You will never really learn any stroke if you rush. Also, follow the lessons in the order they are given here. I have presented them in this order because this is the easiest way for you to learn the strokes.

► IF YOU HAVE PLAYED A FAIR AMOUNT OF TENNIS

Even if you have played a good bit, you can still acquire a smoother, easier game by learning my *method* — which uses the whole body instead of just your arm.

Whether you wish to work on all your strokes or simply to improve one of them, follow the same procedures described above under "If You Are a Beginner." If you wish to work on only one stroke, you would still do well to read the lessons covering the other strokes. Be sure to read the three chapters in Section 1.

► IF YOU ARE AN ADVANCED PLAYER

The chapter, "Subtleties for the Advanced," in Section 3, is especially for you. However, to comprehend my METHOD, you should still read the three chapters of Section 1.

► STUDY THE ILLUSTRATIONS

The illustrations in this book are an *integral part* of each lesson. They are not here just to "liven up" the text. I have tried to make them the next best thing to my actually being on the court with you. Studied carefully, they should help you see exactly how each stroke is to be executed.

► IF YOU OR THE TEACHER IS LEFT-HANDED

Since there are far more right-handers than left-handers, the instructions given here are for right-handed people. If you are left-handed, simply reverse all instructions—for the student, the teacher, or both — for hands, feet, and other parts of the body.

Important Word To Coaches, Friends, Parents or Relatives!

▶ **Do NOT criticize the learner . . .**

Instilling confidence in his ability to learn is all-important. If you cannot say something GOOD about a particular shot or practice bit, DO NOT SAY ANYTHING.

Corrective pointers, offered in a friendly, pleasant tone and approach ARE useful. But DO NOT, under any circumstances, say, "That was terrible!"; or "You're not trying"; or "A six-year-old could do better than that!" — and all similar derogatory statements.

Pointing out gently, calmly, and in a friendly tone what the student has forgotten, or what mistake he is making, is effective. But if you can't say something nice or constructive, DON'T SAY ANYTHING. If you can't take this approach, forget the whole thing. The learner would be better off working with someone else!

The best way to teach ANYTHING is by praising and instilling confidence. You *cannot teach* by tearing down the learner in any way!

Important Preliminaries
for the Six Lessons

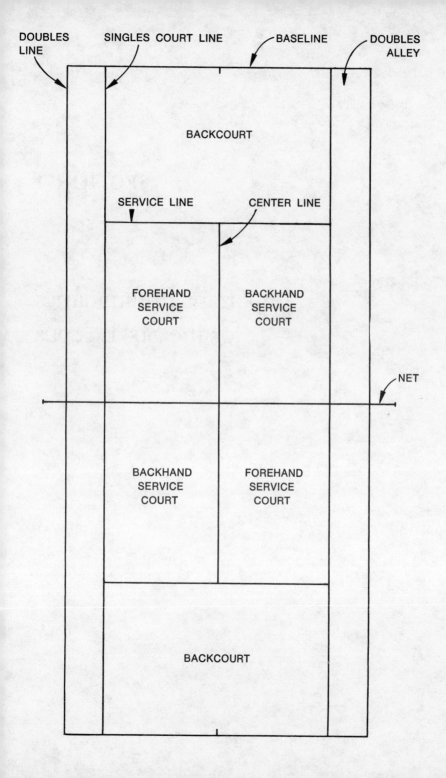

Before You Begin

► Tennis is a BODY GAME, not an arm game

To the casual observer, it appears to be an arm game, and the uninstructed or poorly instructed player will play it that way. When properly played, however, the WHOLE BODY is employed in the execution of each stroke. *Each stroke* has a timed beginning, a middle, and an end. The degree of success I will have with you is the degree to which I am able to get you to employ your WHOLE BODY in the execution of each stroke. If the entire body is employed, then the muscular effort required to execute each stroke is shared by the entire body. This results in grace, power, effectiveness, all-over muscle tone, and a long companionship with the game of tennis.

► Power comes with grace

Grace is achieved through muscular control and timing. Timing is the regulation of time, for maximum smoothness, in performing a physical action. Grace — or agility and smoothness — in tennis comes from the exact timing of the racquet and body movements in relation to the position of the ball. Power does NOT come from a spasmodic or unnecessary flexion of the muscles. Such use of the muscles becomes, in the end (and early!) too difficult for the results achieved.

► TENNIS IS A BODY GAME

The whole body should be employed to get the ball over the net and into the opposite court. This is logical because the human arm at the elbow is not constructed to withstand a continuous, hour-after-hour hacking away. Therefore, to use that portion of the arm too much is folly. This abuse, I am certain, is what has given rise to the ailment known as "tennis elbow."

► Let me assure you of this . . .

IF you will learn to put your whole body behind each delivery, you will not only benefit by exercising your whole body, but you will be able to play this wonderful game of tennis all your life long. I will say that if you play with just your arm, you will be one of those who gives it up and says, "I used to play but now my poor elbow hurts" . . . etc., etc.

When your entire body is used, all — or nearly all — of your muscles come into play at one time or another. Thus, the muscle tone of your entire body is improved. This leads to a flatter "tummy," to better posture, to a greater control of all your muscles, to an increased litheness or suppleness, and to an improved general feeling of health and well-being.

► TENNIS IS A BODY GAME

This is the *basic premise* of this book. All the following lessons and practice methods are planned to help you get your BODY against the ball. COUNT ONE! Each of the tennis strokes has varying *beats,* but *only* ONE COUNT; that is, once a stroke has begun it must flow in a continuous, unified movement.

Approaching the subject in this way has produced innovations in teaching and innovations in practice. You should bear in mind that I am a *teaching* tennis professional. My authority comes from my years of trying to instill these basic principles into the minds of my students and from there into their muscles so that the actions and reactions become automatic.

Thus, when I repeat the basic essentials many times, bear with me. They are so *important,* so *basic,* that I MUST be sure you do not miss them. This book is intended not just for reading, but for TRYING OUT AND PRACTICING with a tennis racquet. Ideally, seek out a friend and do it in pairs—one to read the lesson aloud, a small section at a time, for two hands are not enough to hold book, racquet, and tennis ball. These lessons and practice methods will do you no good unless you try them and assure yourself that they do work.

The lessons and practice methods are designed so that you can make use of them working with a coach, or with a friend, parent, or other relative — whether or not he or she knows how to play tennis.

There is no reason why two individuals, neither of whom knows anything about the game, cannot learn together "from scratch" to play a good game of tennis. All that is required is that you read carefully, and FOLLOW the lessons and suggested practice METHODS EXACTLY as they are given. And then, PRACTICE, PRACTICE, PRACTICE!

Make like a cat on the court —
use your whole body. You'll be happier!

Basic, Basic Points

▶ Tennis is a BODY GAME — not an arm game

The whole body should be employed to get the ball over the net and into the opposite court. The degree of success I will have with you as a student is the degree to which I can induce you to *put your entire body behind each of your movements and each of your strokes.*

▶ Using your WHOLE BODY does *not mean using all the muscles all the time*

If you have learned properly, you will *use only those muscles you need,* when you need them. But proper training of your body will mean that you can call on them WHEN you need them, and they will respond — the way you want them to.

The cat is perhaps the best example of this. Nearly all cats have good muscle tone, and therefore good command and control of all their muscles all the time. But they use ONLY those muscles they need at any particular moment. Consider, for example, a cat stalking a grasshopper. The cat will crawl or walk as slowly or as rapidly as is necessary to get within range of the grasshopper. When it comes TIME TO POUNCE, then, and ONLY THEN, will the cat gather all her muscles together to LEAP on the insect. By constant exercise and use of each muscle as she needs it, the cat always has all the muscles that she needs in perfect condition. This is how a cat achieves that constant grace, agility, litheness, and smoothness.

LEARNING TO PLAY TENNIS WITH YOUR WHOLE BODY can give you the same muscular control — the same muscle tone, suppleness, agility, and grace. It's nothing more than training and using all your muscles, so that each responds *when* and exactly *how* you need it.

► **You never fully face the net when executing any of the five strokes that comprise the entire technical skill of the game of tennis**

This statement is connected with the fact that tennis is a BODY game. While a ball is coming toward your court and you are moving toward the ball, you will turn your body toward the side (away from the net) *as much as possible,* so that you can RE-TURN your body *"through"* the ball as you make your stroke.

The only time you have to prepare yourself to receive a ball is the interval between its leaving your opponent's racquet and its returning bounce on your court.

If you design *always* to utilize this time to prepare yourself, you will always be in position to make your own strokes as well as possible.

► **Never drop the racquet face below the hand holding the racquet**

Get down for low balls by bending your knees. Excellent strokes of tennis are done with a level body pivot — *not* with a vertical swing.

Later, as you acquire more experience and skill, you will discover that there are a *few times* when you need to let the racquet face fall below the hand holding the racquet. But, in general, this is a good rule to follow.

Preparation for the First Lesson

► THE FIVE STROKES

The technique of the game of tennis consists of five strokes, or ways of getting the ball across the net and into the opposite court. These strokes are: the Forehand, Backhand, Volley, Overhead Smash, and Serve. The WAY you execute these strokes makes for your ENTIRE technical ability as a tennis player.

The following series of lessons includes, for each of the five strokes, a technical explanation of the stroke, detailed instructions for learning the stroke, the best ways of practicing with a partner or by yourself, and constant reminders of the basic *things to remember* in connection with each. By the time you finish this book, if you follow the steps and directions carefully, you should have the framework on which to construct, WITH MUCH PRACTICE, a fine game of tennis.

► THE GRIP INDICATOR

Because the *way* you hold — or grip — your racquet is a basic part of my METHOD of teaching you, prepare your hand for the GRIP INDICATOR (you can do this at home, before you begin the first lesson):

On the first finger of your right hand, put a small spot about ⅛″ to ¼″ in diameter (use ink, paint, lipstick, or colored nail polish) in the EXACT LOCATION on your finger shown in Figure 1.

·*(If you are LEFT HANDED, put this spot on the first finger of your LEFT hand.)*

THIS SPOT IS YOUR GRIP INDICATOR!

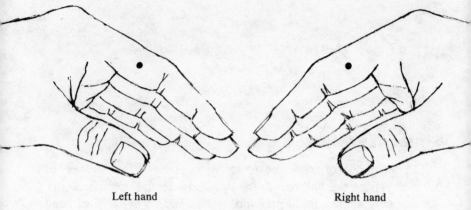

Left hand   Right hand

FIGURE 1

► THE FOREHAND GRIP

To prepare your racquet so that you can easily tell when you are holding the racquet properly with the FOREHAND GRIP, do this:

1. Put your racquet on the floor, the ground, or a table.

2. Directly down the *middle of the widest and flattest part* of the handle (starting at the base) draw a thin, straight line with some material that is easy to see, OR affix a narrow (about ⅛″ wide) strip of adhesive or similar tape. See Figure 2.

3. NOW, pick up the racquet near its throat with the thumb and first finger of your left hand, and grip the handle LIGHTLY with your right hand so that the spot on your finger is EXACTLY TOUCHING the center of the line or tape on the racquet, making sure that your hand is near the bottom of the handle. The spot on your finger MUST be touching the line on the handle. See Figure 2.

THIS IS YOUR FOREHAND GRIP!

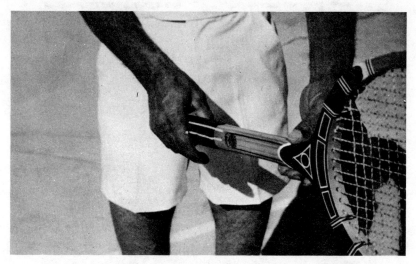

FIGURE 2

Alternative Method for Finding Proper Forehand Grip:

If you don't want to mark a spot on your hand and put a line on your racquet, do this:

1. Hold the racquet by the throat with the thumb and first finger of the *left* hand.

2. NOW, take the lower part of the handle in your *right* hand, and — while the weight of the racquet is still being held by the left hand — with the first finger of your right hand FEEL FOR THE BROAD PLANE of the racquet handle so that your finger is touching it. Place the bottom joint of the palm side of your first finger as nearly parallel to the broad plane of the handle as possible (see Figure 2). The *center* of this joint *must* be on the *center* of the *broad flat area* of the racquet.

EITHER WAY that you arrive at it, this is your FOREHAND GRIP, which you can learn to *feel* at once. If properly held, there will be a slight gap between the handle and the place where your thumb joins your hand.

> NOTE! If you have played tennis before, this is probably NOT the way you were taught to hold the racquet. IF you are holding the racquet as I want you to, your hand will be a LITTLE FARTHER to the LEFT of the handle (or right, if you are left handed) than you are accustomed to. This difference is IMPORTANT!

FIGURE 3a

When this grip is properly held, and you hold the racquet straight out in line with your *left* foot, you will see that the racquet face has become an extension of the flat palm of your hand. The edge of the racquet should form a *perfect right angle* with the surface of the court or with the ground. See Figures 3a and 3b.

▶ THE BACKHAND GRIP

To prepare for the backhand grip, draw another line or place another ⅛″ wide strip of tape along the center of the *first bevel* to the *left* of the flat, wide part of the handle (that is, on the bevel to the left of the line for your Forehand Grip). See Figure 4. If you are left handed, put the line along the center of the first bevel to the RIGHT.

You will use this line, together with your Grip Indicator (the spot on your finger), when you learn the Backhand Grip in more detail a little later.

FIGURE 3b

FIGURE 4

► PREPARATION ON THE COURT

Always take a position in the middle of the court.

This has a bearing on the central strategy of ALL tennis. If you have stroked a ball at a point away from the center, you don't wait to see what is going to happen to the ball. You get back to the *center* because that is the spot from which you can best move for your next stroke.

NOW, take your position just behind the *baseline* in the *exact center* of the court (that is, half way between the left-hand and right-hand side lines).

► THE READY POSITION (See Figures 5a and 5b)

1. Weight equally on both feet, facing the net, feet about one foot apart.

2. Thumb and forefinger of left hand holding the racquet at its throat and supporting its weight; edge of racquet pointed toward your imaginary (or real) opponent.

3. Right hand in proper FOREHAND GRIP position, holding the racquet LOOSELY. For comfort, the handle may slant slightly to the right (or left, if you are left-handed).

ALWAYS RETURN IMMEDIATELY TO YOUR READY POSITION AFTER EACH STROKE — DO NOT STOP TO ADMIRE YOUR LAST SHOT!

► PRACTICING MOVING FROM THE READY POSITION

From your Ready position, move to your right, turn and pretend to stroke a ball, then return *immediately* to your Ready position in the center of the court. Repeat the maneuver to your left side. Continue alternating to the right and to the left, always returning to your Ready position in between each stroke. Your objective in this practice is to make the quickest return possible to the center and to your Ready position. Each time, try to step and reach a little *further*. Remember, tennis is a BODY GAME!

FIGURE 5a

FIGURE 5b

NOW, LET'S LEARN THE FOREHAND STROKE!

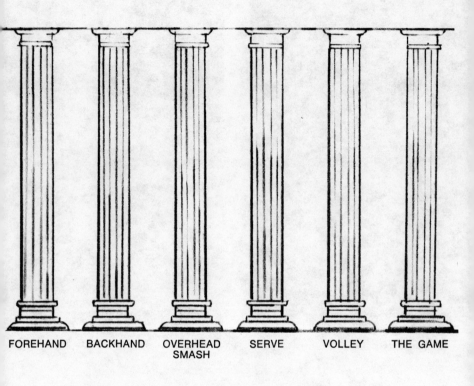

FOREHAND BACKHAND OVERHEAD SERVE VOLLEY THE GAME
SMASH

These are the pillars that hold up your game —
make sure they are the best quality,
then build your tennis "house" on them!

Six Lessons – Strokes and Game

The Forehand Stroke

► **MOVEMENT OF THE STROKE**

Beginning from your Ready position, the head of your racquet is carried behind you, *edge* of the racquet face passing *near* your right shoulder, the racquet straight up and down (perpendicular to the ground). The racquet makes a curve *down* to a flat plane behind you, so that the edge of the racquet is parallel with the ground, and then is *moved forward on this flat plane* (or, in other words, is *moved forward on the straight line on which you want the center of the racquet face to meet the ball*), and is moved "through" the ball, and finally rises to finish with the right hand holding the racquet at shoulder height and the top of the racquet pointing skyward — *in one CONTINUOUS motion.*

► **MOVEMENT OF THE BODY**

As you perform this maneuver with the racquet, the body and feet turn to the *right side,* so that the body can RE-TURN "through" the ball, and so that the leading foot (*left*) can step sideways *toward* the net at the time of the stroke, thus adding body power, momentum, and weight to the stroke. This is about what a good right-handed baseball player does when batting.

► **FOUR BEATS TO THE STROKE**

There are FOUR BEATS to the total motion of stroking the ball on the Forehand (or on the Backhand), but only ONE COUNT because, *once the racquet starts,* its movement is CONTINUOUS and does NOT stop until the finish of the stroke — which is with the racquet pointing skyward over your *left* shoulder.

NOW — LET'S DO THIS WITHOUT A BALL:

Take your Ready position (see Fig. 6) just behind the baseline in the center of the court, and let's go through the beats of this stroke. Practice this in SLOW MOTION. Check your GRIP INDI-CATOR!

As you start your turn to the right, you will pivot on the *ball* of the *right* foot and your *left foot* will swing into line with the right. The weight remains on the *right* foot until you stroke the ball.

Beat 1: As you turn (Fig. 7), your racquet is still straight up and down (perpendicular to the ground) because this is the way you expend the least energy, and, as you turn, the racquet will turn with you, still supported at the throat by the thumb and forefinger of the left hand.

Beat 2: The left hand releases the throat, and the racquet, still perpendicular, passes behind you CLOSE to the right shoulder (Fig. 8).

Beat 3: When the racquet (still perpendicular) has arrived at its ultimate point behind you (Fig. 9), the wrist and extending elbow begin curving the racquet face further *behind* and *down* to its position on the plane or line on which you wish to meet the ball.

Beat 4: The arm — *the fingers are now gripping the racquet tightly* — swings forward parallel with the ground (Fig. 10) to meet and *pass "through"* the ball with *locked wrist* and body pivoting. The arm *follows through* on this motion until the racquet top is pointing skyward over your left shoulder (see Fig. 11).

IMPORTANT: During all of Beat 4, use your ENTIRE arm and shoulder — NOT your elbow!

FIGURE 6

FIGURE 7

FIGURE 8

FIGURE 9

FIGURE 10

FIGURE 11

▶ LEARNING THE FOREHAND STROKE WITH A PARTNER

If you have a friend or the coach to work with, the easiest way to learn this movement is to start with the Four-Beat position and work back gradually, until you are doing the complete One, Two, Three, Four beats with ONE count — or in ONE CONTINUOUS movement.

1. Take the BEAT 4 position (Fig. 12). Face the right side away from the net (your left hip pointing toward the net). Hold your arm with the racquet stretched behind you (edge of the racquet parallel with the ground), the wrist broken back slightly. Weight on your *right* foot. Your friend will take a position *two good paces* directly in front of you, and *one good pace* toward the net (see Fig. 13). He will hold the ball in his left hand, palm facing down, with arm extended toward you and at head height. KEEP YOUR EYES CONSTANTLY ON THE BALL.

2. Your friend will release the ball so that it DROPS (he does *not toss* it!), and after it has struck the ground and starts rising, you will swing your racquet forward in its straight line, to meet and pass "through" the ball (Beat 4), continuing the motion until the racquet is pointing skyward over your left shoulder. Your friend should say "Four" as the released ball strikes the court.

As you start your swing for the ball, tighten the fingers; your wrist will pull the head of the racquet forward even with the hand. Tightening the fingers will lock your wrist through your elbow to your shoulder muscles (deltoid), and the ball will be propelled primarily by virtue of your left foot stepping *netward* in the direction you wish the ball to go, *and* by the body pivot at the same time. Be sure to "follow through" to the finish of your stroke.

Immediately before and after passing "through" the ball, the entire body is under its maximum muscular tension. That is, during this BEAT 4, there is a *deliberate tightening* of the muscles.

HINT: If you're having poor success hitting the ball because it is coming too close to you, have your friend move a *little* further away; if the ball is much too far away from you, have him move a *little* closer. But, always *reach for the ball* as much as you can.

FIGURE 12

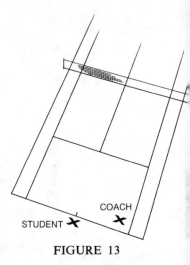

COACH

STUDENT

FIGURE 13

3. After some success propelling the ball (3 or 4 minutes), take the BEAT 2 position (see Fig. 14), exactly the same as FOUR except that the racquet is held perpendicular to the ground, and the head or top, CLOSE to your right shoulder, feet apart but parallel with the net and with each other. Left thumb and forefinger are still holding the racquet by its throat. Check your GRIP INDI-CATOR! Your friend is still standing in the same place. *Your eyes are on the ball* which he is holding up, just as before.

Now, he slowly chants "Two-o-o," as you begin SLOWLY moving the racquet perpendicularly behind you (your left hand lets go as you begin this count). On "Three-e-e," you curve the head of the racquet further back with the wrist and down into its position with the edge of the racquet parallel to the ground. On "Four" your friend will DROP the ball and you will drive it (stroke it) forward as described above when we started with Beat Four. Remember, the movement is *continuous*. KEEP YOUR EYES ON THE BALL.

FIGURE 14   FIGURE 15

4. When you can do this fairly well (3 or 4 minutes), then start at the Ready position facing the net (Fig. 15), with your friend still standing in the same place. Check your GRIP INDICATOR. Now, fasten your eyes on the ball and, as your friend *slowly, slowly, slowly* chants "One-e-e, Two-o-o, Three-e-e, Four," go through the whole turning and stroking movement of the Forehand. Your friend still DROPS the ball on "Four."

At first do the beats in SLOW motion, then *gradually* pick up speed on the beats. But, as you pick up speed, be sure to keep your motion *continuous and smooth* from the beginning of Beat 1 until the completion of the follow-through at the end of Beat 4.

5. After this practice with your friend becomes easier (4 or 5 minutes), have him move up close to the net — but still on the same side with you — while you remain just behind the baseline in your Ready position. Check your Grip Indicator. Your friend is

now going to toss balls to you. For the first four tosses *only,* he will help you by saying "Start" just before he tosses. At this point you will *begin* the Forehand movement you have learned. After the *first four* tosses, the thrower will *no longer* say "Start," and you will find your own timing. The tosser says "start" only to remind you that MOST of your body movements — except Beat 4 — are done while the ball is *in the air* coming toward you.

The tossed ball should land 6 to 8 feet *in front* of you, and 6 to 8 feet *to your right.* At first, your friend should toss *softly* and *slowly.*

▶ TIMING

Here is the TIMING you want to acquire on this practice movement: The *instant* the ball is thrown toward you, begin your Forehand-beat movements (ONE, TWO, THREE). You will have arrived at the beginning of FOUR by the time the ball has *struck the court* in front of you. Start your level BEAT 4 swing aiming at the point where you *guess* the ball will arrive. At the same time, step sideways toward the net with the left, or front foot, which will arrive in line with the ball at the same moment that the racquet face contacts the ball.

This netward movement will accomplish three things:

1. **It will tend to flatten the racquet face to meet the ball correctly;**

2. **It will somewhat *fix* the ball in the air for the instant of impact;**

3. **It will put your entire *body weight* against the ball — provided the fingers of the racquet hand are *tight* enough while passing "through" the ball. This bypasses the elbow and ties onto your shoulder muscles. (Remember — Tennis is a body game, *not* an arm game!)**

When this last practice method is even partially mastered, drop the preliminary practice methods and concentrate entirely on this one — that is, on your continuous ONE, TWO, THREE, FOUR-beat swing and on TIMING your swing to the flight of the ball. Keep your EYES ON THE BALL!

► SELF-PRACTICE METHOD —
FOREHAND PRACTICE WITHOUT A PARTNER

Stand in your BEAT 2 position, facing the right side (your left hip pointing at the net), racquet face at your right shoulder, left arm extended downward with the hand palm up holding the ball. Lift your left arm up, TOSS the ball UP *above* your head (the higher the better) so that it will bounce an arm-and-a-racquet length in front of you and one *good* step toward the net.

Remember to keep the fingers holding the racquet *tight* long after contact with the ball (8 to 12 inches afterwards), until the ball has entirely left the racquet face. At the same time, try to stay *with* the ball with the racquet face as long as possible by sliding the left foot in the direction you wish the return flight of the ball to take. In other words, COMPLETE THE FOLLOW THROUGH!

> Tossing the ball *above* your head will give you time to train your racquet arm and your body in their TWO, THREE, FOUR-beat stroke. Arranging to have the ball strike the court *toward* the net from you will allow you to practice moving the lead *(left)* foot into a line with the ball as you stroke it.

REMEMBER!

- **KEEP your EYES on the BALL.**

- **CHECK YOUR GRIP INDICATOR.**

- **Make the motions of the four beats ONE CONTIN-UOUS MOVEMENT — do NOT stop once you have started. Even if you think you made a mistake some-where along the way, keep the motion CONTINUOUS.**

- **HANG LOOSE until BEAT 4.**

- **Follow through! Do NOT stop your motion when the racquet meets the ball. *Finish* your stroke.**

► PLAYING

It is only one step more now to standing in the backcourt and stroking the ball with a graceful, continuously executed stroke. If you have someone to play with who knows how to play, or if your friend has been learning with you, you can now actually start stroking the ball back and forth across the net.

Any time when two players are learning together, use the SELF-PRACTICE METHOD for getting the ball into play. Both of you should be in the center of your courts, back at the baseline. One of you gets in the Ready position; the other uses the Self-Practice Method to get the ball into play. Try to see how well each of you can go through your Four-Beat movement and return the ball to your opponent, each of you assuming the Ready position as soon as you have completed a stroke. Discovering that you can actually hit the ball back and forth will give you a feeling of confidence.

For this kind of practice:

1. *All* balls are to be put into play using the Self-Practice Method;

2. Both players should be deep in their courts — well behind baselines.

For the quickest mastery of all the strokes, NEVER hit a sloppy shot, even to get a ball over to your opponent who is waiting to serve. Instead, *use* the Self-Practice Method. The sooner your stroke becomes a conditioned reflex action, the sooner you can give your entire attention to playing the game of tennis with strategy and greater pleasure. At this time you may be said to *own* your stroke.

Always work for perfect TIMING. Work for the sometimes-attainable ideal of perfect strokes and perfect timing. In actual play and hitting practice, you will learn to synchronize your body movements in getting to the ball with the timing of your Four-Beat stroke, shortening or lengthening it as the time available to you requires.

The Backhand Stroke

► MOVEMENT OF THE STROKE

The Backhand Stroke, like the Forehand, begins in the Ready position, facing the net. The head of the racquet is carried to your *left* behind you, held CLOSE to your body and perpendicular to the ground. The racquet describes a curve *down* to a flat plane behind you, so that the edge of the racquet is parallel with the ground, and then is *moved forward on this flat plane* (or, in other words, is moved forward *on the straight line on which you want the center of the racquet face to meet the ball*), is moved "through" the ball, and finally rises to a finish with the hand holding the racquet shoulder high, and the top of the racquet pointing skyward.

► MOVEMENT OF THE BODY

At the same time that you perform this maneuver with the racquet, the body and feet turn to the *left side,* so that the body can RE-TURN "through" the ball. The leading foot *(right)* steps *netward* into line with the ball at the time of the forward stroke. This is called "stepping into your shot." The motion adds body momentum, power, and weight to the stroke. This is about what a good left-handed baseball batter does with body and with his right foot when he wishes to hit the ball with power. With the baseball batter, however, the *turn* is not involved, because he already *knows* on which side he is going to take the ball.

[35]

► FOUR BEATS TO THE STROKE

As with the Forehand, there are FOUR BEATS to the total motion of stroking the ball on the Backhand, but only ONE COUNT because, *once the racquet starts,* its movement is CONTINUOUS and does NOT stop until the finish of the stroke — which is with the racquet pointing skyward over your *right shoulder.*

NOW — LET'S DO THIS WITHOUT A BALL:

Take your Ready position (see Figs. 6 and 15) just behind the baseline in the center of the court, and let's do some detailed study and practice of the Backhand movement. In the beginning, do each beat in VERY SLOW MOTION.

IMPORTANT! In your Ready position, your right hand still holds the racquet LOOSELY in the *Forehand grip.* (Check your Grip Indicator!)

Beat 1: Your racquet is still perpendicular to the ground (straight up and down) because this requires the least energy. Start your turn to the left (Fig. 16), and, as you pivot on the ball of the *left* foot, bring the *right* foot slowly around parallel to the left foot for balance. Keep your weight on the *rear* or *left* foot by keeping the heel of the *right* foot raised. As you turn, the racquet will turn with you. You still support it at the throat with the finger and thumb of the left hand.

Beat 2: Take the racquet, still perpendicular, behind you CLOSE to the *left* shoulder (Fig. 17). Your left thumb and finger are *still* supporting the racquet at its throat.

Beat 3: When the racquet has arrived perpendicularly at its ultimate point behind you (Fig. 18), the left hand will lower the racquet *further* behind in a *curve downward* into its position with the racquet edge parallel to the ground. (NOTE: During this beat the thumb and forefinger of the *left* hand turn the racquet slightly in your *right hand.* (See "TURNING TO THE BACKHAND GRIP" below.)

FIGURE 16   FIGURE 17   FIGURE 18

FIGURE 19   FIGURE 20

Beat 4: The right arm swings out — racquet edge parallel to the ground — to meet and *pass "through"* the ball with *locked wrist,* body pivoting, and *right* foot stepping sideways *netward* (Fig. 19). At the point of contact with the ball, the *right* ELBOW *must* have turned under and *must point* toward the ground. This locks the arm and the racquet to the shoulder. As in the Forehand, the arm follows through until the racquet points skyward (Fig. 20). IMPORTANT! During all of BEAT 4 use your entire ARM AND SHOULDER — not your elbow.

► TURNING TO THE BACKHAND GRIP FROM THE FOREHAND GRIP

As you begin the beats, try to keep the LOOSEST possible grip on the handle with your *right* hand — so loose that the whole handle will turn *easily* in your hand. Now, as you bring the racquet head *around* and down behind you (BEAT 3), *with the thumb and fore-finger* of your *left* hand turn the face of the racquet FLAT toward the oncoming ball. *Then* tighten your grip on the handle with your right hand. You will find that you have automatically gotten the proper Backhand grip. This assumes that your left hand has brought the racquet around and down into its hitting plane parallel to the ground, and, at the same time, that it has flattened out the face of the racquet toward the oncoming ball BEFORE you tighten the grip of the right hand on the handle of the racquet.

Alternate Method (Manual):

The second choice for getting the Backhand grip from the Fore-hand grip is this:

As you are making your turn for the Backhand stroke, with the left thumb and forefinger at the throat of the racquet, you simply turn the racquet handle in your right hand *one turn* to the right. Be sure the racquet turns IN your hand. At the same time you feel for your proper grip with the same portion of your right forefinger that is YOUR GRIP INDICATOR (see Fig. 1).

In other words, *someplace* during the time your body is turning to the left, *turn* your Forehand grip to the Backhand grip, using the left hand to do the turning and the right hand to *feel* for the grip. You will find that the most natural place to turn to the Backhand grip will be when you lay the racquet head back and down into the hitting plane of your stroke — that is, on the straight line on which you want the center of the racquet face to meet the ball.

► MOVEMENT OF THE FEET

Beat 1:   As you start your turn, raise your *left* heel and pivot to the left on the ball of your *left* foot (Fig. 21a).

FIGURE 21a   FIGURE 21b   FIGURE 21c

Beat 2: Now, bring your right foot around in line, parallel with the left one, the right heel slightly raised — so that a straight line connecting the toes of both feet would, if extended, hit the net (Fig. 21b).

Beat 3: Weight is on the *left* foot, giving the right foot freedom to move forward. Your racquet is being lowered back and down into its hitting plane or line (see Fig. 21b).

Beat 4: The right foot moves toward the net and in line with the projected flight of the ball (Fig. 21c).
On this Beat 4 you have *shoved* with your left foot and *stepped netward* with your right. This stepping toward the net has added much of your *body weight* to the ball, and, combined with the simultaneous turn of the shoulders and torso, has given *body impetus* (push) to the ball.

▶ LEARNING THE BACKHAND STROKE WITH A PARTNER

With a friend's help, the easiest way to teach your body this Backhand stroke is to begin with the BEAT 4 position, and then add on beats, working backward, until you are doing the complete

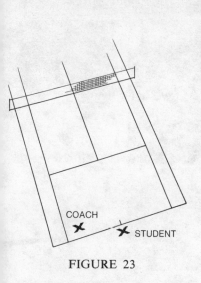

COACH

X ————**X** STUDENT

FIGURE 23

FIGURE 22

ONE, TWO, THREE, FOUR BEATS with ONE count — or in ONE CONTINUOUS movement.

1. Take the BEAT 4 position (Fig. 22). Face the left side away from the net (your right hip pointing toward the net). With the right hand, hold your racquet extended behind you to your left, the edge parallel to the ground, wrist broken slightly, and with the BACKHAND GRIP. Your friend will take a position *two good paces* directly in front of you, and *one good pace* toward the net. (See Fig. 23.) He will hold the ball in his right hand, palm facing down, with the arm extended in front of him at head height. KEEP YOUR EYES CONSTANTLY ON THE BALL.

2. Your friend will release the ball so that it DROPS (he does *not* toss it!), and, after it has struck the court and starts rising, you will swing your racquet forward in its straight line (edge parallel to the ground) movement, to meet and *pass "through"* the ball (Fig. 24 — BEAT 4 point of impact), continuing the motion until the racquet is pointed skyward over your right shoulder.

[40]

FIGURE 24   FIGURE 25

Tighten your fingers and start turning your elbow under as you start your swing for the ball. Your wrist will pull the head of the racquet *forward* even with your hand. Tightening the fingers and turning your elbow under will lock hand and racquet to the shoulder muscle (deltoid), and the ball will be propelled primarily by virtue of your right foot stepping netward in the direction you wish the ball to go, *and* by the body pivot — or the turn of the upper part of the body at the same time (Fig. 24). NOTE: At point of impact elbow points *downward*. Be sure to "follow through" to the finish of your stroke.

Immediately before and after passing "through" the ball, the entire body is under its maximum muscular tension. That is, during this BEAT 4, there is a *deliberate tightening* of the muscles.

3. After some success propelling the ball in this way (3 or 4 minutes), take the BEAT TWO position (Fig. 25). The racquet is perpendicular to the ground, and the top is CLOSE to your left shoulder. Left thumb and forefinger are still supporting the racquet by the throat. Your right hand is holding the handle *loosely* in the

Forehand grip. Your friend still stands in the same place. *Your eyes are on the ball* which he is holding up, just as before.

Now, he slowly chants "Two-o-o" as you begin moving the racquet perpendicularly behind you, "Three-e-e" as you lower the racquet head *further* back and down into its position with the edge parallel to the ground. The thumb and forefinger of the left hand are still supporting the racquet at its throat. *Now,* this thumb and forefinger turn the face of the racquet FLAT toward the oncoming ball. On "Four-r-r" your friend will DROP the ball, and you will stroke it toward the net as described above when we began with BEAT 4. KEEP YOUR EYES ON THE BALL.

4. When you have succeeded in *blending* the TWO, THREE, FOUR beats (3 or 4 minutes) start at the beginning of BEAT 1 — that is, in the Ready position facing the net (Fig. 26). Your friend still stands where he has been. Now, fasten your eyes on the ball, and as your friend *slowly, slowly, slowly* chants "One-e-e, Two-o-o, Three-e-e, Four-r-r," go through the whole turning and stroking movement of the Backhand. Your friend still DROPS the ball on

FIGURE 26   FIGURE 27

"Four." At first do the beats in SLOW motion, then gradually pick up speed on the beats. BUT, as you pick up speed, *be sure* to keep your *motion continuous and smooth* from the Beginning of BEAT 1 until the completion of the follow through at the end of BEAT 4 (Fig. 27).

5. After this practice becomes easier (4 to 5 minutes), have your friend move toward the net on the center line — but still on the same side of the court with you (Fig. 28) — while you remain just behind the baseline in your Ready position. Check your Grip Indicator. Your friend is now going to toss balls to you. For the first four tosses *only,* he will help you by saying "Start" just before he tosses. At this point you will *begin* the Backhand movement you have learned. After the first four tosses, the thrower will *no longer* say "Start," and you will find your own timing. NOTE: ALL of your body movements — except BEAT 4 — are done while the ball is in the air coming toward you and before it strikes the court.

The tossed ball should land 6 to 8 feet *in front* of you, and 6 to 8 feet *to your left.* At first, your friend should toss *softly* and *slowly.*

▶ TIMING

Here is the TIMING you want to acquire on this practice movement: The instant the ball is thrown toward you, start your Backhand-beat movements (ONE, TWO, THREE). You will have arrived at the beginning of BEAT 4 by the time the ball has *struck*

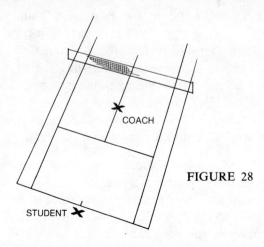

COACH

STUDENT ✘

FIGURE 28

the court in front of you. Start your level BEAT 4 swing aiming at the point where you *guess* the ball will arrive. At the same time, step sideways toward the net so that your *right* foot will be coming into line with the ball when you stroke it (see Fig. 23). KEEP YOUR EYES ON THE BALL.

This stepping forward into line with the ball will accomplish three things:

1. **It will tend to flatten the racquet face to meet the ball correctly;**

2. **It will somewhat *fix* the ball in the air for the instant of impact;**

3. **It will put your entire *body weight* against the ball — provided the fingers on the racquet head are *tight (elbow turned toward the ground)* while passing "through" the ball. This bypasses the elbow and ties onto your shoulder muscle (tennis is a BODY GAME!) Remember that ELBOW!**

When this last practice method is even partially mastered, drop the preliminary practice methods and concentrate entirely on this one — that is, on your continuous ONE, TWO, THREE, FOUR-beat stroke and on TIMING your swing to the flight of the ball. KEEP your EYES on the BALL.

AT LAST, stand in the backcourt, your partner with his racquet in the opposite backcourt. Work for the sometimes-attainable ideal of perfect strokes and perfect timing. In actual play and hitting practice, you will learn to synchronize your body movements in getting to the ball, and the FOUR-BEAT, ONE-COUNT stroke of your racquet. You will learn, also, by practice, to shorten or lengthen the beat of your stroke to accommodate it to a fast or to a slow ball.

TRY IT NOW! Have your friend throw you a fast ball. Simply narrow the whole pattern of your ONE, TWO, THREE, FOUR BEATS until the whole pattern is performed in less space and time, and SEE WHAT HAPPENS! You hit the fast ball back in perfect timing, using *mostly* your *body*.

IMPORTANT! The pattern of the FOUR BEATS of the stroke must be adjusted to the speed of the oncoming ball. Obviously, with a fast ball each of your four beats must be performed in less time and space. That is, on Beats 1 and 2, the racquet does not go as far behind you. On Beat 3, the curve downward is less; and Beat 4 is shortened in time and space.

BUT, the same bodily muscular movements and tensions are maintained as with a stroke where you have time to take a large swing.

► SELF-PRACTICE METHOD — BACKHAND PRACTICE WITHOUT A PARTNER

Hold the racquet with the Backhand grip. Take your BEAT TWO position, facing the left side *away* from the net (your right hip pointing at the net), racquet face at your left shoulder. Hold a ball in your left hand extending past and just above your right arm, pointing toward the net (your arms are CROSSED), hand PALM UP (Fig. 29). Lift your left arm up, TOSSING the ball

FIGURE 29

above your head — the higher the better — so that it will bounce an arm-and-a-racquet length in front of you and *one good step* toward the net.

Tossing the ball *above* your head will give you time to train your racquet arm and your body in their TWO, THREE, FOUR-BEAT Backhand stroke. Arranging to have the ball strike the court *toward* the net from you will allow you to practice moving the lead foot into a line with the ball as you hit it.

Remember to keep the fingers holding the racquet handle *tight* long after contact with the ball (8 to 12 inches afterwards), until the ball has entirely left the racquet face. At the same time, try to keep the ball "in" the racquet face as long as possible, by sliding the right foot in the direction you wish the return flight of the ball to take.

The next step in self-practice is to aim at targets in the opposite court: the corners, the alleys, the baseline, and so on. When you begin to aim at targets, keep checking the quality of your stroke. The real reason for this practice is to perfect and own the stroke.

REMEMBER!

- **KEEP your EYES on the BALL.**

- **Make the motions of the four beats ONE CONTIN-UOUS MOVEMENT. Do NOT stop once you have started. Even if you think you made a mistake some-where along the line, keep the motion CONTINUOUS.**

- **HANG LOOSE until Beat 4.**

- **With the Backhand, on contact with the ball the elbow of your racquet hand MUST be pointed toward the ground. *This is the whole secret of the Backhand.***

- **Follow through! Do NOT stop your motion when the racquet meets the ball. Finish your stroke.**

▶ PLAYING

It is only one more step now to standing in the backcourt and stroking the ball with a graceful, continuously executed stroke. If you have someone to play with who knows how to play, or if your friend has been learning with you, you can now actually start stroking the ball back and forth across the net, using the Backhand and Forehand.

Always use the Self-Practice Method for getting the ball into play. Try to see how well each of you can go through your FOUR-BEAT movement and return the ball to your opponent, each of you assuming the Ready position as soon as you have completed your stroke. Discovering that you can actually hit the ball back and forth, and that you have two strokes at your command, will give you a strong feeling of confidence. REMEMBER, you are working on your stroke and your timing.

For this kind of practice:

1.   All balls are to be put into play using Self-Practice Method;

2.   Both players should be deep in their courts — well behind the baselines.

For the quickest mastery of the strokes, NEVER hit a sloppy shot, even to get a ball back to your opponent who is waiting to serve. Use, instead, the Self-Practice Method. The sooner your strokes become simply a conditioned reflex action, the sooner you will be able to disregard the mechanics of your strokes, and you then may be said to *own* them.

Then, you can give your entire attention to the joyous challenges of outwitting your opponent. Tennis is somewhat like chess: in it, probabilities, psychology, geometry, and their infinite variations become pieces in the game.

The Overhead Smash

► WHEN TO USE THIS STROKE

Here is the situation that calls for the Overhead Smash stroke:
Your opponent has hit a "short" ball — that is, not very deep into
your court — and you have come forward to return it. After stroking
it back, you have chosen not to go back to the baseline but to
continue *forward* toward the net position — 10 or 12 feet back from
the net.

REASON:

- Once you are up near the net, retreat is both difficult and
  unwise. The closer you are to the net the wider the angle at
  which you can place the ball. This gives you an advantage. See
  illustration below.

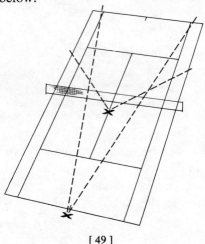

► READY POSITION

Your Ready position is the same as before (see Fig. 23) —
squarely facing the net, the top of your racquet head high, left thumb
and forefinger supporting the racquet at its throat, *loose* grip with
your right hand on the handle, edge of racquet pointed toward your
opponent, racquet perpendicular to the ground — EXCEPT that
the racquet handle should be almost fully extended out in front of
you (Fig. 30).

FIGURE 30

Your opponent now has only three ways to win the point from
you. He can pass you at the net by hitting his ball down either
of your sidelines, or he can "lob" the ball over your head.
Your answer to the "lob," or high ball, is the OVERHEAD
SMASH.

► MOVEMENT OF THE STROKE

The movements of the Overhead Smash stroke are like those of an overhand baseball pitch. *Try it now*. Put your racquet down. Take a ball in your right hand. Pretend you are in the Overhead Smash Ready position by extending both arms toward the opposite fence of the court. NOW, swing the ball down and throw it forcefully against that target.

Did you notice that you turned your body to the side, swung your arm first *down*, then *up* behind you in a pendulum swing, dropped your hand to your right shoulder, then — starting with your wrist — that you flung the ball over your head and out from you, at the same time pivoting your body with the throw to give added impetus (push) to the ball? That was the motion of the OVERHEAD SMASH. *Now*, repeat the same motions with your racquet in your hand instead of the ball.

► GRIP

The ideal grip for the Overhead Smash is the *Backhand Grip* (see Fig. 4), because:

1. The Backhand Grip is also used for the Serve, so your Overhead Smash practice will also benefit your Serve;

2. Using the Backhand Grip trains you to turn your wrist to *flatten the racquet face* as it contacts the ball — another necessity while serving.

You may find this grip uncomfortable at first, and, since you hit the ball directly in *front of you* (not always so with the Serve), you can use any grip *between* the Forehand and the Backhand grips, but never anything *beyond* the Forehand Grip — that is, your right hand must NEVER be further to the right on the handle than it is for the Forehand grip.

Since we are now working for fine strokes, TRY your best to use the Backhand Grip. The sooner you learn this grip, the sooner you will be able to perfect your stroke.

FIGURE 31   FIGURE 32

► THREE BEATS TO THE STROKE

There are THREE BEATS to the movement of the Overhead Smash stroke, but ONLY ONE COUNT, because the movement is continuous.

Beat 1:   Swing the racquet *down* like a pendulum and *up* behind your head (Fig. 31).

Beat 2:   Drop the racquet loosely behind you so that it passes over your *left* and then your *right* shoulder blades ("scratch your back"), by releasing ALL the muscles — including elbow muscles — of your arm and wrist (Fig. 32).

Beat 3:   As the racquet falls in its circular motion, use the wrist to "throw" the flat face of the racquet at the ball, beginning with the wrist and following with the arm and the RE-TURN of your body "through" the ball (Fig. 33). The stroke finishes with the racquet down behind your *left* side (Fig. 34).

FIGURE 33   FIGURE 34

This is the movement and the BEAT you will use whether you wish to hit the ball *easy* or *hard;* whether you have a "cinch" shot or a difficult one. It is the *accomplishment* of the WHOLE MOVEMENT that makes the Overhead Smash a *body* stroke. The TURN and RE-TURN of the body, synchronized with the CONTINUOUS-BEAT movement of the arm, is your insurance of a long and happy life with the game.

► THREE THINGS TO REMEMBER ABOUT THE OVERHEAD SMASH

1. *Catch the ball about a foot and a half in front of your head* as you look toward the net (Fig. 35). Catch it in the center of your flat racquet face with the tip of the racquet slightly bent over the ball.

REASONS:

▪ You have more control of a ball struck or met in front of you.

FIGURE 35

- The Overhead Smash is the *one* ball which you can always hit *down* on safely. Catching the ball in front of you makes this DOWN-stroke natural.

- Ideally, you will want to *fall against* the ball with your *body* weight. Hitting in front of you helps makes this body fall possible. *Remember:* Tennis is a BODY GAME. Your racquet travels *over your head* in a *straight* line to the ball. You only complicate things and slow your meeting with the ball if you swing the racquet in a curve.

2. *When you strike the ball, EXTEND your racquet arm FULLY* (Fig. 36). In other words, reach as high in the air as possible and meet the ball at FULL arm's length.

REASONS:

- By meeting the ball with an extended arm, you bypass the elbow and *lock onto* the body through the large shoulder muscles. Therefore, you can use your body *re-turn* and *fall* to give impetus (push) to the ball.

■ If you meet the ball with a bent elbow, you tend to bevel (turn slightly on edge) the face of the racquet too much. If you have miscalculated, and have allowed the ball to come too low, it is *better* to drop to your *knees* to take the ball at arm's length, rather than to hit with a bent elbow.

3. *When you start the "throw" of the racquet* — the THREE-BEAT MOVEMENT — your *entire left side* (left ankle, left hip, and left shoulder) *will be turned toward and in line* with the ball (Fig. 37).

FIGURE 36

FIGURE 37

REASON:

- The Overhead Smash, at its best, involves a *coil* of the body and a *re-coil* on the ball. That is, a *turn* of the body *away* from the net and a *re-turn* "through" the ball.

  When your opponent first sets up the "lob," you will be squarely facing the net. The first thing to do is line up your *left* side, head, and shoulder with the ball. During any further maneuvering, KEEP your left side pointed toward the ball, until you "throw" your racquet head at it as described in the THREE-BEAT movement. With practice, you will learn to synchronize your TURN, your RE-TURN of the body, and the THREE-BEAT racquet movement of the Overhead Smash.

► **THREE THINGS TO KNOW AND REMEMBER ABOUT THIS THREE-BEAT, ONE-COUNT, CONTINUOUS MOVEMENT**

1. On the ONE BEAT, as the racquet head swings *down* and *up,* use as little muscle power as possible. Give the head of the racquet a start down by pushing with the thumb of the left hand, and have the racquet swing like a pendulum *down* and *up* behind you.

REASON:

- There is no need for muscle power. Conserve it. Concentrate on timing. Also, this loose, pendulum-like initial swing helps promote the *smoothness* of the stroke, where the REAL power lies.

2. On the THIRD, or "throw-the-racquet" BEAT, move the face of the racquet in as straight a line as possible over your head. To accomplish this, start the racquet face moving toward the ball with your wrist.

REASON:

- The Overhead Smash ball will be *right in front of your head.* You reach the ball quicker and pinpoint it in the air by going in a straight line for it. This is why the shot is called the "over (your) head smash."

3. The wrist NEVER locks on this stroke.

Beat 1: On the swing down, the *wrist* is *loose.*

Beat 2: On the drop, the *wrist* is *loose.*

Beat 3: On the "throw," the unlocked wrist STARTS the head
of the racquet forward, continues its forward movement
through impact with the ball.

At *impact* there is the GREATEST POSSIBLE MUS-
CULAR TENSION throughout the whole BODY. The
arm is straight up, moved by the shoulder muscles, and the
body — ideally — is falling forward and pivoting
"through" and "over" the ball. The wrist at contact with
the ball takes up the shock, the fingers tight around the
handle, but the wrist is still moving the head of the racquet
"through" and OVER the ball.

▶ OVERHEAD SMASH IS THREE CONNECTED, LOOSE "FLOPS"

It actually helps to think of the THREE BEATS as three connected loose "flops":

1. "FLOP" the racquet *down* and *up* behind you while loosely
   turning your body.

2. RELEASE all tension on the arm and let the racquet "flop"
   behind your back, your wrist to your right shoulder.

3. "FLOP" the racquet face into and over the ball while re-
   coiling the shoulder and body in its RE-TURN "through"
   the ball. There should be bodily tension only at the moment
   of impact (striking the ball).

NOW — LET'S DO IT!

▶ LEARNING THE OVERHEAD SMASH WITH A PARTNER

1. Take your Ready position for the Overhead Smash in the
center of the court, about 5 or 6 feet back from the net. Hold the
top of your racquet head high, your arms extending the perpendicular (straight up and down) racquet *almost* full length in front
of you (see Fig. 30).

NOW, turn to your *right* with your feet (point the left hip at the tosser), but *keep* your racquet extended toward the net in the same position.

2. Your partner will stand in the other court *facing* the net. His best position is 3 or 4 feet back from the net and 8 or 10 feet into the court from the net post on his left (Fig. 38). This insures that the natural turn of your body will carry the smashed ball *away* from him (provided *you* are right-handed — if left-handed, your partner should reverse his position).

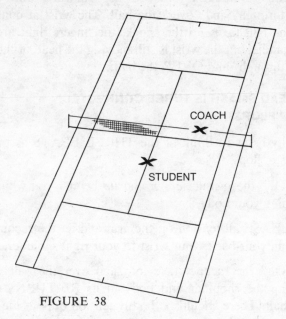

FIGURE 38

3. Your partner will hold a ball down low, palm of his hand facing UP. He will TOSS (underhand toss) the ball up into the air 2 or 3 racquet lengths directly ABOVE your head. He should try AT FIRST to make the shot as easy as possible for you.

4. As he swings the ball *up,* you will start your ONE, TWO THREE-BEAT movement, knocking the ball into the opposite court.

When you have had some success with this (2 or 3 minutes), square up your feet toward the net — that is, *point* your *toes toward* the net — in your Overhead Smash Ready position. This next step will be easier because it is more natural.

NOW, the *second* your partner tosses the ball up into the air, begin your ONE-BEAT movement and accompany it with a step with your LEFT foot (to turn your *left* hip towards the ball) pointing your *left ankle* toward the ball in flight.

Beat 2: Drop arm and racquet to your right shoulder.

Beat 3: SMASH the ball into the opposite court with the final RE-TURN of the whole body *"through"* the ball. On the end of this movement, your *right* foot will swing forward.

Do this for 3 or 4 minutes until you can do it fairly well.

NOW, play a little game. Every time you are successful in hitting the tossed ball back into the opposite court, take a step backward in your court to receive the next ball. Try always to OVERDO your TURN (impossible!) and RE-TURN "through" the ball. You will be happily surprised by your success with this! Soon you will find yourself deep in your own court hitting high overheads. THEN, return to your original position at the net and start over again. You will find quickly that you have gained a great deal of confidence by this procedure.

For all future practice with a partner, *eliminate* the "turn-to-right" stance in Step 1 (that was the confidence builder), and ALWAYS from now on begin practice on this stroke with the Overhead Smash Ready position (see Fig. 30).

HOWEVER, to warm up adequately, ALWAYS start every practice session (with a partner) near the net. Then *gradually* move back into your court. Ask your partner to make his tosses more and more difficult for you. Let him try to get the balls over your head, or toss the balls to fall somewhere to your right or to your left. In this way, you can *practice maneuvering your body into its proper position while the ball is in transit.*

The Overhead Smash is the easiest stroke of all to come by, or to "own." It is the most satisfying, and also one of the most important in tennis, because it gives you much confidence when you are in the front part of your court.

If you "own" only a Forehand and Backhand, you are not sure of yourself when you get up to the net. But if your opponent tries to "lob" the ball over your head and you "put it away" with a good Overhead Smash, he has less confidence about trying the "lob" again.

The Overhead Smash is the easiest of the strokes to come by and "own" because your proficiency in it bears an almost mathematical relationship to the amount of correct practice you do.

REMEMBER!

- **Line the ball up directly in front of your head as you look toward the net.**

- **Do all your maneuvering BEFORE the ball arrives.**

- **HANG LOOSE throughout this important stroke.**

- **The wrist NEVER LOCKS.**

- **KEEP your EYES on the BALL.**

- **CATCH the ball in the center of the racquet face.**

▶ SELF-PRACTICE METHOD — OVERHEAD SMASH PRACTICE WITHOUT A PARTNER

Here is a method that will give you practice on the ONE, TWO, THREE-BEAT movements and on maneuvering for the ball:

1. Hold the ball at shoulder height in your left hand, fingers pointed downward, arm completely extended. Hold your racquet (with the Backhand grip) with the racquet DOWN underneath the ball, with the flat face toward the ball, and both arms extended.

2. DROP the ball and come up under it with the flat racquet face, knocking the ball skyward vigorously 30 to 40 feet into the air.

Practice maneuvering so that the ball comes down in a straight line with your *left* shoulder and about 1½ feet in front of your head.

3. Just as you *hear* the ball strike the ground *start* your ONE, TWO, THREE-BEAT movement, and on the THREE BEAT you will find the ball in front of you in the perfect hitting position.

► TIMING

This must be exact. Knock the ball into the air. Point your racquet toward it, and *never taking your eyes off it,* maneuver so that the ball comes down by your left shoulder. The *instant* you hear the ball hit the court, start your ONE, TWO, THREE-BEAT movement.

You will be able to get a great deal of practice out of this, and it will help you to master the Overhead Smash. The better way is, of course, to have the balls tossed to you. Lacking a partner, however, the Self-Practice Method is a very good substitute. Because this is a very strenuous stroke, I recommend that, if you have balls tossed to you, you practice this stroke *no more than TEN MINUTES at a time*. If you practice by yourself, knocking the ball up in the air affords you the necessary respite, and you need not watch the time.

The Serve

The Serve is hit with the same ONE, TWO, THREE-BEAT movement as the Overhead Smash and is, in essence, the same. This is why the Serve lesson follows the Overhead Smash. The problem of the Serve is that you must synchronize the *ball toss,* which you do yourself, with the ONE, TWO, THREE-BEAT swing of your racquet. (You will find later that the two somewhat-detached movements come together on the TWO BEAT; don't worry about it now.)

If you will take *one step at a time* in this lesson, complications will fall away. The result will be a fine ONE-COUNT SERVE, wonderful to look at, wonderful to do, and employing the whole body in the sweeping motion of the stroke. If you can place the tossed ball where you wish it to be, at a SLOW pace, this will simplify the rest of the Serve motion.

> *If you can toss the ball where you wish it to be, you can serve; if you can serve, you can play tennis.*

The ball toss is the pacesetter of the Serve, so let us now and hereafter make the *hand* holding the ball for the toss the *timer* of the whole Serve operation.

The Serve lesson will start, then, with the ball toss and we will add on one movement after another until you are performing the complete Serve. So, FROM THIS POINT ON, DO NOT INTERRUPT THE SEQUENCE OF THIS LESSON.

THE TOSS OBJECTIVE: To take the ball in a deliberate, undeviating pattern from a front position *slowly* down and then to put it up in front of you to a spot about 15 inches away from the body and one-arm-and-one-racquet-length high. This spot is located in the air between the left shoulder and the left eye. The toss must be slow enough to allow the body time for its smooth, flowing movements, and the two motions, body and toss, must flow together before the ball is struck. It will take time and practice to train the "ball tosser" (you and your hand). In the future, if anything goes wrong with your Serve, look first to your toss for flaws.

▶ STEP 1 — THE TOSS

Put your racquet down and take a tennis ball in your left hand. Take a position just behind the baseline and just to the right or left of the center marker of the court. Point your entire left side — ankle, hip, and shoulder — toward the small service court *diagonally* across the net from you. Extend your left arm, shoulder high, holding the ball toward the indicated service court in your *upturned palm* (Fig. 39). In the *slow,* continuous BEAT of ONE, TWO, take the ball, with your fingers extended, down to a point about 15 inches in front of your left knee (Fig. 40), then raise your hand *straight up* — slightly faster now — as HIGH as your hand can reach, so that the ball *rises off* the platform formed by your hand at the TWO BEAT. The ball should rise an arm-and-a-racquet length above your head and be about 15 inches in *front* of you as you face the right side of the court.

Always make your ONE BEAT slow, but if you want increased height for the ball, simply increase the speed of the TWO. BEAT. The motion of the toss does *not* stop between the ONE and TWO BEAT; it is continuous.

Valuable things to remember for the ball toss:

1. Throughout the whole movement, keep the palm of your ball-tossing hand UP.

2. Do *not* allow the ball to leave your hand until the hand has reached its maximum height.

FIGURE 39   FIGURE 40

3. As you begin your ONE-BEAT movement of swinging
    the hand and ball down, move your eyes away from the
    opposite service court UP to a spot where you intend the
    tossed ball to be. Your eyes will fasten on this spot before
    the ball arrives. *This is the most valuable hint of all,* because
    you are likely to be able to toss the ball to a *point* at which
    you are looking.

When you are able to put the ball about where you want it almost
every time, you are ready for:

► STEP 2 — THE SERVE READY POSITION

Pick up your racquet in your right hand and assume the same
position you had for the toss. Stand erect with your weight on both
feet. NOW, holding the racquet in a *loose BACKHAND* grip, extend
your racquet out until the flat face of the racquet is touching the ball.
RELAX the muscles of the arm and those of the entire body as much

FIGURE 41   FIGURE 42

as possible. Fasten your eyes on a spot in the opposite service court at which you are aiming racquet and ball (Fig. 41).

This is your READY POSITION for the SERVE.

> Learn to take your time here. Remember, the game cannot begin until you put the ball into the opposite service court. UNTIL that moment, you are in command. Take time to concentrate.

▶ STEP 3 — SWING

NOW, beginning in your Serve-Ready position, in the BEAT of ONE, TWO, swing your racquet down, up, and drop it *loosely* behind your back, your wrist at your shoulder just as you did on the Overhead Smash (Figs. 42, 43a, and 43b). DO NOT RELEASE BALL (forget about the ball-tossing hand for now!).

FIGURE 43a   FIGURE 43b

Do this swing-drop 8 or 10 times, concentrating on looseness, particularly of elbow and wrist, during this TWO BEAT.

▶ STEP 4 — HIP TURN-BODY TURN

As you swing your racquet down into your ONE, TWO BEAT, turn your hips as far to the *right* as possible. This will serve to raise the heel of your left foot, bend the left knee, and shift your body weight to your right foot. At the same time that your hips turn, your shoulders *will also* turn to the right. As they do, *raise* the left shoulder and *drop* the right one (see Fig. 42). Do *this* 8 or 10 times: ONE, TWO; ONE, TWO; ONE, TWO. . . . NOW, add on Step 5.

▶ STEP 5 — COMBINATION OF TOSS AND SWING

Now, as you swing your racquet down into its ONE BEAT — turning your hips and shoulders — swing your left hand with the ball down and up, as we learned before, but *do not* release the ball. Your hand will arrive at its highest point at BEAT TWO, as your racquet drops behind your back (see Fig. 43a). Here we go! ONE, TWO — racquet and ball go *down* together; hips turn, shoulders turn, racquet moves up and behind your head, dropping at TWO, while the ball-tossing hand has arrived at its ultimate height. ONE, TWO; ONE, TWO; ONE, TWO. . . . Do this 8 or 10 times. NOW, add on Step 6.

▶ STEP 6 — EYES

Take your Serve Ready position. Hold your eyes on some spot in the opposite service court where you want the ball to go. As you begin your ONE-BEAT motion, move your eyes from the opposite court to a spot where you wish the tossed ball *to be* and fasten them on this spot, while you go through the previously gained ONE, TWO movements. Do this 8 or 10 times.

NOW — LET'S SERVE THE BALL!

▶ THE COMPLETE SERVE

Address the court in your Serve Ready position. Swing through all the BEATS and, when you are satisfied with them, release the ball from the platform of your hand, as you have practiced, and — BEAT THREE — literally "THROW" the face of the racquet at the ball, the stroke finishing as the racquet passes down past your left side. Now, release the ball every time, and do this with 10 or 15 balls. These are the essential outlines of the Serve. Now, let's analyze further the whole movement. (See Figs. 44a through 44e.)

▶ THE POSITION AT IMPACT

The *reason* for these ONE-, TWO-BEAT movements on the Serve is simply to get the body and racquet into the best hitting position. Look at it. At the end of the TWO-BEAT position, the left arm with ball is raised to its maximum height, left shoulder is up, right shoulder is down; back is partly turned toward the net. Your racquet is hanging loosely behind your back, wrist *loose* and gathered at your right shoulder, left knee bent, left heel raised, body weight on the

FIGURE 44a

FIGURE 44b

FIGURE 44c

FIGURE 44d

FIGURE 44e

right foot (see Fig. 43a). Your eyes are fastened on the spot where you wish the tossed ball to be. Are you not in a perfect position to "throw" the racquet face at that spot?

► RACQUET MOTION AT POINT OF CONTACT

When you "throw" the racquet face at the ball (THREE-BEAT), you will attempt to "catch" the ball in the *center* of the face, slightly on *top* of the ball and slightly on the *right-hand side,* or away from you (see Fig. 44e). The racquet face will pass *over* the right-hand part of the ball, giving the ball a spin from bottom-left edge to upper-right edge.

(NOTE: *first* contact with the ball MUST be made with the *flat* surface of the racquet!)

In flight, that is the way the ball is tumbling, and so the ball has two arcs to perform: (1) The fact that the ball is spinning from left side to right will arc the ball from right to left into the court; (2) the ball is also spinning from *bottom* to *top,* and this spin serves to arc the ball *up* and *down* into the court. With a judicious mixture of these arcs, the tallest, shortest, weakest, or strongest player can design to hit the ball with all his strength and still depend on it arcing *into* the opposite service court.

► BALL TOSS LOCATION

Why is the ball to be tossed brought back down to a point between the left shoulder and your chin, and then taken up in a straight line from this point? Study the SEMICIRCLE your racquet face travels on the 'throw" or THREE BEAT. Begin at the TWO-BEAT position, and in SLOW motion start the racquet face on its way, stopping it at the point where you would want to contact the ball.

You will see that at this point the racquet *face,* with a slight turn of the wrist, is *flat,* whereas at other points in its travel it is *beveled.* More important, at this point of contact you will see that you still have half of your body RE-TURN to give to the ball, whereas if the ball had been placed toward the net, you would have used up *all* your body RE-TURN *before* contacting the ball. After contact with the ball, of course, the racquet face continues its semicircular sweep down, and finishes behind you on your left.

► SERVE PRACTICE WITH PARTNER

While you serve, have your partner consult the book to check on your body movements.

NOW, serve the ball, concentrating on the whole ONE-COUNT, THREE-BEAT movement. You will be delighted to see many of these balls arc over the net and into the opposite service court. Remember, once motion starts, it does *not* stop until the stroke is finished. Try now to forget the various steps by which we arrived at this Serve. Think of it as a *single movement* (which it is) and get a feeling for the whole of it. Most of all at this point, *concentrate* on LOOSENESS.

► DIFFERENT TYPES OF SERVES

There are almost infinite variations on the spin that the service ball can be given. These variations are all primarily dependent on where, on its semicircular path, the racquet face meets the ball. This governs the mixture of the two arcs which you give the ball. Some of these variations are: the extreme *bottom*-to-*top* spinning ball — the American Twist, hit behind your head; the extreme *side*-to-*side* spinning ball — the Slice, hit to the side; the *practically-not* spinning ball — the Cannonball, hit in front (this power ball is hit in front — toward the net from you; for SERVE MASTERY, learn the Serve taught in this lesson FIRST); and all the variations which lie between. The Serve I have tried to give you is not only a fine beginning Serve, in that it combines in almost equal parts the two spins that control the Serve ball, but it is also probably the most *effective*. Best of all from our standpoint, it makes the most use of the *re-turn* of the body "into" and "through" the ball (power).

► SELF-PRACTICE METHOD —
SERVE PRACTICE WITHOUT A PARTNER

Collect as many old tennis balls as you can for your practice sessions. PRACTICE YOUR SERVE REGULARLY! As with the Overhead Smash, your mastery or "ownership" of the Serve is almost mathematical in its relationship to the number of correctly hit balls. The following are points to watch when you practice:

1. Vary your hitting speeds. You learn more by trying to do the whole action in slow motion than you do by trying to hit hard all the time. With this method you are training yourself in TIMING, that is, always performing the full *body* and *arm* actions at changing speeds.

2. Always cultivate *looseness:* ONE, TWO, THREE BEATS — "FLOP, FLOP, FLOP." If there is a hitch, you are doing it wrong, so check back in this chapter. If you hurt beyond the simple soreness of previously unused muscles, you are doing something incorrectly. Check back in the book for the Six Steps involved in learning the ONE, TWO, THREE-BEAT movement.

3. If your balls are going too deep into the opposite court, check your *bottom*-to-*top* spin on the ball, which controls your up-to-down arc. You are probably not giving your ball enough bottom-to-top spin. To cure this, be sure the *face* of the racquet travels skyward UP the back of the ball to give it more bottom-to-top spin. This can also be done by the *body rising,* so that the face of the racquet is traveling up and over the ball.

4. If the balls are going too short, you are giving the ball *too much* bottom-to-top spin. Hit the ball flatter.

5. If your balls are going too far to either side of the target service court, check the position in the air at which you are contacting the ball. This position should be generally in line with your left shoulder and the right corner of your court. If the ball is being struck too far in front of this point, it will have a tendency to strike to the left of the opposite service court. If the ball is struck too far behind this reference point, your ball will have a tendency to fall to the right of the target service court. Also, you may be meeting the ball with the face of the racquet beveled. Check your grip, AND check the position of your wrist at contact with the ball.

6. Arrange — with the turn of your wrist beginning with the THREE-BEAT motion — to have the face of the racquet perfectly flat. At this point, the *advantage* of holding the racquet with the Backhand grip appears: If you have met the ball while holding the racquet in the Backhand grip, you now have "wrapping" power or leverage left in the wrist to "wrap" the face *over* and *around* the ball.

7. If, in your first practice sessions, you find the *full* Backhand grip *too* uncomfortable (since you have not yet trained your wrist to turn the face flat), try holding a grip somewhere *between* the Backhand and Forehand grips — say half way. But *always* conscientiously work to adapt your service to the use of the full Backhand grip, for the best future service.

8. The wrist NEVER locks during the Serve. To show yourself how loose the wrist must be during the Serve motion, take an old, worn-out racquet or a sturdy stick in your hand. Take the Serve-Ready position. Go through your full Serve motion, only this time FLING the whole racquet or stick as far away from you as you can. Repeat the process. Did you notice how loose the wrist was? This is the degree of looseness the wrist must cultivate for the Serve, because during the Serve you are actually "throwing" the racquet face away while holding on to the handle.

9. As your confidence grows in your Serve practice routine, teach yourself to concentrate during the Serve motion on certain particular things that are part of the Serve. One of these is: "Center the ball in your racquet face." As you address the court in your Serve-Ready position, shut out all things from your mind *except,* "Center the ball." Say to yourself during the whole motion: "Center the ball, center the ball, center the ball!". . . .

10. When you become adept at hitting the service court on the other side of the net, pick out corners and spots IN the other court to try to hit. Set increasingly more difficult tasks for yourself. Devise and set up targets in the other court to hit. Make games within games.

With regular practice, following the above method, you will be delighted with your progress in mastering the Serve. Even more happily, you will find that, as in chess, each step only opens up new possibilities to exploit.

FOREHAND VOLLEY ▶

◀ BACKHAND VOLLEY

The Volley

A Volley is the return of a ball before it strikes the ground, when the ball is not high enough to be dealt with as an Overhead Smash. Also, the Volley is used primarily near the net where you are in the "aggressive" position. According to the rules of tennis, the only ball which you *must* let strike the ground before hitting it is the ball being served to you. After the served ball goes into the proper court and the ball is "alive," you may deal with it without having to let it hit the ground.

The Volley is given to you last in this series of lessons because its technique bears little relationship to the other four strokes. The Forehand and Backhand are related in their movements; in general they are the same stroke done on opposite sides of your body. The Overhead Smash and the Serve are certainly first cousins, if not brother and sister, in their close relationship. As I said in the beginning of these lessons, the technique of the Forehand is similar to the action by a right-handed baseball batter; that of the Backhand resembles the movement of a left-handed batter. The technique of the Overhead Smash is similar to the action of a vigorous overhand pitch, and so is the Serve.

The movement, or technique, of the Volley most resembles that of a fencer or swordsman. The ideal Volley movement is done in the BEAT of ONE, like the foot-shoulder-body jab of the fencer.

In this lesson we are going to learn the "Block-Chop" Volley. There is another Volley, and a very effective one, known as the "Stroke" Volley. But in my opinion, the "Block-Chop" Volley is the better way of dealing with the ball in the Volley position, and it is certainly the best way to get the entire body into the stroke. The "Stroke" Volley may be added to your game later, if you feel the need of it.

► POSITION IN THE COURT

Stand 12 to 14 feet back from the net in the center of the court for all beginning practice. At start of the Volley this is the ideal location — get used to it.

► THE VOLLEY READY POSITION

The Ready position for the Volley is the same as that for the Overhead Smash: racquet head high, racquet held perpendicular (straight up and down) almost at full arm's length in front of you (Fig. 45). I might say here that the closer to the net you get, the higher and further in front of you the racquet should be held. When you are at the net you will handle returning balls to either forehand or backhand from the 'same Ready position.

► THREE IMPORTANT THINGS TO REMEMBER ABOUT THE VOLLEY

1. *Meet the oncoming ball as far in front of you as possible* — that is, as far as your lead foot (left foot for the Forehand Volley, right foot for the Backhand Volley) can *step* and as far in front of you as you can *reach* your racquet (Fig. 46).

REASONS:

- You have more control of an oncoming object if you contact it well in front of you. The closer it approaches, the less maneuverability you have. The ball coming over the net in Volley position is at its height the instant it passes over the net. A fraction of a second later, when it is on your side of the net and has dropped to, say, net height, the return shot is slightly more risky. You are now more apt to hit the net with the ball. Another fraction

FIGURE 45

FIGURE 46

of a second later the ball has dropped below the net and now to return it effectively takes one of the most difficult shots in tennis. You will see that the closer to the net you "take" the ball the better chance you have for a safe and effective return.

2. *On the Volley there is NO backswing and little follow through of the racquet face.* It is a ONE-BEAT movement.

REASONS:

▪ There is no backswing because you do not have time for it. You utilize your time best here by simply presenting the flat face of your racquet to the oncoming ball and sharply *blocking* it. Furthermore, you do not need great power to win a net point. At the net you have extreme angles open to you and it is placement that will most likely win the point for you. There is no reason to "over-win" the point by pulling back into the hard-hitting position in this situation, especially since a fast-returning ball can catch you unready if you do.

▪ There is no follow through of the racquet face because, having returned the ball with a ONE-BEAT, block-chop movement, you do not need one. Your whole commitment is on the ONE-BEAT, block-chop, and when the ball leaves the racquet face the movement is finished. Also, in the unlikely event that your opponent is in position for a quick return, your racquet face will have made an unnecessary move if you follow through. It is better use of time to return to the Ready position for another Volley or Overhead Smash.

3. *To handle a low Volley, close to the ground, NEVER drop the face of your racquet below the hand holding it.* As you bend your knees, bring the racquet *down,* but keep its face higher than the hand to meet the ball (Fig. 47), lead the bottom edge slightly and use the same block-chop movements and body extensions (see Fig. 47) as on a better-positioned ball. This is applicable to any low ball handled as a Volley. Even if your hand holding the racquet is touching the court, keep the face of the racquet slightly higher at contact with the ball.

REASONS:

- If you are properly extended forward and down, it is physically awkward to drop the racquet face below your hand.

- Control with the racquet face, which is what you want here, is much greater in this position.

- Your wrist is in its best position for locking, with the racquet face slightly above your hand.

If you will use this method for handling low Volleys, you will be happily surprised how easy it becomes to return this low shot.

Now that you have read the three important things for you to *know* and *remember* in general about the Volley, let's begin the actual lesson and you can refer to these points again from time to time. For this lesson you must bring a friend to the court with you, for the simple reason that it is impossible without him. Have your friend stand on the other side of the net with a bucket of balls.

FIGURE 47

FIGURE 48

▶ FOREHAND PRACTICE — PRELIMINARY PRACTICE

Without your racquet, take a position in the middle of your own court, about 12 or 14 feet back from the net. Face the net squarely, weight even on both feet. Extend both arms toward the net as if you held a racquet in the Volley Ready position (Fig. 48). Now have your partner toss *easy* balls, aiming a few inches to the right of your shoulder. You catch the balls in your right hand as far in front of you as you can *step* with your left foot and *reach* with your right arm and hand. *Really stretch out!*

The idea is to prevent the ball from approaching one *fraction* of an inch closer than you can help. *Now* you feel the action of the Forehand Volley. As you have probably noticed by now, the *left foot* movement is very important. Notice that *while* the ball is progressing toward you, you are stretching toward it.

After a few minutes of this practice, read the next material on the Forehand Volley and *then* pick up your racquet.

▶ FOREHAND VOLLEY — MOVEMENT OF THE STROKE

Using the Forehand grip, the movement of the Forehand Volley is as follows: The *wrist* of the hand holding the racquet will drop the face of the racquet to the right, about in line with your hand, and at the same time flatten it toward the oncoming ball. Extend the arm. By this time the *left* foot has started forward, and the ball is met and JOLTED by the almost-flat face of the racquet *and* by the body moving forward. If there is any feeling of passing "through" the ball, it is that the racquet face, after meeting the ball, passes down on it. This is the slight "chop" of the block-chop. Do not overdo it. The ball should have left the face fast, and too much down-chop will take speed from the ball. Try to feel in this shot how the step — almost STOMP — of the left foot sends the ball back over the net.

CAUTION:

- The action of the elbow is at a minimum here. You begin your Ready position with the arms almost completely outstretched. Then the face of your racquet is flattened and dropped into position with your wrist. Further action on the ball is performed by the body moving *forward* to meet and jolt the ball. *Avoid bending the elbow; avoid pulling the racquet back.* Long years of teaching have taught me that this will be your tendency at first. Beware of it! Say to yourself, "ALL movement is forward!"

NOW — LET'S DO IT!

Take your Volley Ready position, racquet in hand, and have your partner *softly* toss you some balls to the same spot as before — that is, 4 or 5 inches to the right of your right shoulder. As you succeed in returning these, keep moving back from the net to make it more difficult for yourself. Always take the Volley Ready position for each ball that is tossed. Do this practice for 5 or 6 minutes until you feel the ONE-BEAT, one-step (LEFT FOOT!), block-chop, arm extended, body-against-the-ball movement.

► LOW FOREHAND VOLLEY

Now ask your partner to toss you some low balls. Make the same Volley movements described above, but this time get *down* to your ball by bending at the knees.

Be sure to keep the face of the racquet slightly above the hand holding it during the entire ONE-BEAT stroke. As you drop the face of the racquet to the right for these low balls, *lead* the bottom edge slightly (that is, have the bottom edge of the racquet slightly more towards the net than the top edge), and as you Block-Chop the ball, taking the strings *down* the back of the ball, you will see the ball *rise* over the net (Fig. 49). What a triumph!

► BACKHAND VOLLEY — PRELIMINARY PRACTICE

Face the left side of the court (right hip and shoulder pointing toward the net), and extend your racquet out from you toward the net as if you held a sword or fencing foil — the edge of the racquet

FIGURE 49

FIGURE 50

pointing towards the net. Hold your left hand high up behind you for balance. Keeping your racquet thus extended, take a series of deliberate steps sideways toward the net; almost STAMP your right foot, shoving with the left, and you will have demonstrated to yourself the ideal movements of the Volley. Now, holding the Backhand grip, do the same action but *this time* bend your wrist so that the flat face of the racquet is facing the net — that is, the racquet face is back even with the extended hand that is holding the racquet (Fig. 50). You will then begin to feel the correct technical action of the Backhand Volley.

► LEARNING THE BACKHAND VOLLEY

Take a position 10 or 12 feet from the net. Stand on the center line, facing the left side of the court with feet close together. Holding the racquet with the Backhand grip, extend your racquet straight toward the net with arm and shoulder in a line (see Fig. 50). Now,

with your wrist, flatten the face of your racquet toward the opposite
court. The face of your racquet will be on a line with, and 2 or 3
inches higher, than the hand holding it. Your left hand and arm
are held straight behind you, shoulder high — for balance. You
are now in the fencer's position except that you are opposing the
flattened racquet face to the ball, rather than the point of your sword
toward your opponent. Bend your head to the left and see if you
can comfortably peer through the flattened strings of the racquet
to look at the ball. If so, you are in the right position. This may be
a bit uncomfortable at first, but never mind; you don't want this
game to be *too* easy, do you?

Your partner will now toss *easy* balls aimed to strike your racquet
face. You meet the tossed ball by simply stepping *toward* the net
and the oncoming ball with your *right* foot, jolting the ball with the
rigidly held face of your racquet and with the forward motion of
your body. Do NOT bend the elbow. Now you have felt the true
Block-Chop Volley.

> Notice that it was mainly the forward movement of your *right*
> foot that propelled the ball, and that the shock was taken up
> by the shoulder and body weight leaning against the ball. If
> you want greater velocity or power on the ball, simply step
> *further* (ONE step only, however!) forward as you meet the
> ball.

Really work at this for a few minutes. The next will be more natural
to you — and therefore easier.

Come back to your Volley Ready position at the net, holding a
loose *Forehand* grip, thumb and forefinger of the left hand supporting the racquet at its throat, edge of the racquet pointed at your
partner. Now, try the following several times "dry" — *without* having the balls tossed at you. Start your turn to the left — the position
you had in the practice immediately preceding this (see Fig. 50),
by swinging the right foot around in front of you. At the same
time that the *right* foot is moving forward into position, turn the
racquet from the Forehand to the Backhand grip by using the thumb
and finger of the left hand to turn it. Remember, it is only a *one-
bevel* turn. The *handle* in your right hand will turn. Avoid turning

the right wrist. *Turn* the *handle* to the Backhand grip, then tighten the fingers on the grip. As your right foot arrives in its front position, your left hand will have turned the racquet to the Backhand grip and this hand then swings behind you for balance, as in fencing. The racquet does not retreat, nor does your right elbow bend back during *any part* of this movement. Beware of this!

After a few of these "dry" runs, have your partner toss balls. You start from your Volley Ready position. He will toss *easy* balls slightly to your left side at the same spot he tossed to in the previous exercise, and you will volley them away.

Following this method you will find the Backhand Volley amazingly easy to master. It seems to be a more natural body movement and, therefore, in general easier than the Forehand Volley.

▶ VOLLEY PRACTICE WITH A PARTNER

After learning these movements, the best Volley practice is for you and your partner (we hope he can Volley too, by this time!) to stand an even distance back from the net and try to keep the ball going back and forth in the air with your Volley strokes. To put the ball into play, get into your Ready position, holding a ball in your left hand. Toss the ball up and out in front of you and slightly to the right of your perpendicularly held racquet. As the ball descends you can practice your wrist-body-foot movement as used in the Volley. (This method is recommended for starting out any Volley practice, or for simply putting the ball into the other court.)

With your partner, Volley back and forth — *very easily* at first. You will find that in a short time a certain rhythm has become established as you get more and more consecutive balls over the net. This is great fun and is almost a game within a game, enjoyable in itself.

The following suggestions will aid you in this Volley practice:

1. After starting this practice with a Volley stroke, *always* return immediately to your Volley Ready position. You will not have any extra time before the ball comes back. If you use your time well and return to the Ready position while the ball is in the air, you are prepared for a return that comes on the opposite side of you from the previous ball. If you are not in the Ready

position, you will have too much to do and not enough time to do it in. Due to the excitement of getting the first balls back and forth, this proper use of time may seem difficult, but with conscientious practice it will become automatic.

2. Be sure you and your partner stay an even distance back from the net. If one of you is even *one* step closer to the net, he has such an advantage that the practice is not the best.

3. Start your beginning practice sessions with easy balls, both of you standing close to the net. As you gain accuracy, move gradually back and make the returns faster. (This comes after MUCH PRACTICE on accuracy.) Do NOT do this at first. Much of the joy is in being able to keep the ball going, and I want you to experience this pleasure.

    For this purpose, make your beginning shot as easy as possible for your partner to return. Plan in advance to Volley Forehand to Forehand, and place the ball where he can easily reach it.

4. After you have managed a good continuous series, try something different. At first, always plan these exchanges with your partner ahead of time, since you want to keep the ball going. Put the first ball to the Backhand and the subsequent shots to the Forehand. Then alternate Forehand and Backhand Volleys. Through this series of progressions you will learn to return to the Ready position between Volleys. It will not matter then on which side of you the ball comes. You will simply, by reflex, perform either the Backhand or Forehand Volley from the Ready position.

The Volley is a real pleasure to master and hours of enjoyable exercise can be gained from it. It is very good in training your eye also. You will be surprised how practice in utilizing these methods will give you possession of the stroke.

▶ SELF-PRACTICE METHOD — VOLLEY PRACTICE WITHOUT A PARTNER

The two-person Volley practice is by far the best, but if absolutely no partner is available, you can gain some benefit by hitting against a backboard. This is NOT recommended at *all* in the early stages of mastering the Volley because the ball returns so fast from the backboard that you will shortcut and incorrectly perform the necessary movement.

If you *must* practice against a backboard, get into your Ready position. holding a ball in your left hand. Toss the ball up and out in front of you and slightly to the right of your perpendicularly held racquet. As the ball descends, you can practice your wrist-body-foot movement as used in the Volley. This method is recommended for starting out any Volley practice, or for simply putting the ball into the other court. You are trying to teach your body a reflex movement, and you can spoil a lot of good practice by making even a few sloppy shots.

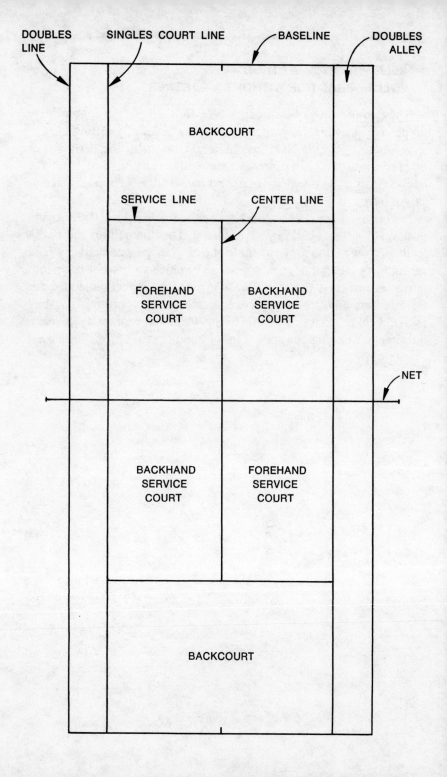

The Game Itself

Tennis is not an "easy" game in which to become skilled. In it there are three physical variables with which you must always cope:

1. On every point *you* are moving;

2. Your *target* is changing;

3. You are trying to stroke a *moving target,* the ball.

Since your target is the part of the court where your opponent is NOT, the target naturally changes as he moves. In most other active games, either the target sits, or the object you are striking or throwing sits until you move it.

However, the *basics* of tennis, like those of chess, can be quickly learned. The fundamental ideas and rules of either game — enough to start playing — can be learned in ten minutes. From that point, you can go on from improvement to improvement, from complexity to complexity without *ever* — and this is the exhilaration for most of us who pursue tennis — *completely* mastering either. In other words, there is enough challenge here to individual capacity for a lifetime.

There will *always* be areas in which you can improve your tennis. The strokes outlined for you in this book are designed to allow you the greatest room for technical improvement no matter how far you wish to progress in the game.

A wonderful minimum objective for you now would be sufficient mastery of the game and strokes to enable you to express your own personality on the court, simultaneously enjoying exhilarating and vigorous exercise. It just happens that the better you play the game, the more you will enjoy it and the more people there are who will enjoy playing with you.

So let's get into the game itself. The object is to put the ball back over the net into your opponent's court one more time than he can return it to you. The game is set in motion with the Serve.

▶ WHO SERVES FIRST?

You or your partner spins a racquet, letting it fall on the court. As it spins, one of you — decided in advance — will call which way the racquet will fall; that is, on which side it will land (there is almost always a difference in lettering or design between the two sides; if not, make a mark with a pencil or with some sharp object on one side of the handle). If the one to call it has named the side correctly — just like "flipping a coin" — he gets his choice of *whether or not* he wishes to serve first. OR, he may elect to choose the side of the court on which he wishes to begin playing. The loser of the spin has a choice of what is left. For instance, if the winner of the spin says, "I'll serve," or "I'll receive," the other player may choose the court in which he wishes to start playing. If the winner of the spin has elected to choose the court, then the loser has a choice of whether he wishes to serve or receive. This choice may be important due to the position of the sun, among other things.

▶ BEST POSITION TO SERVE

The rules state that to begin each game one player must serve into the Forehand service court of his opponent, and that, when doing this, the server must stand behind the baseline and to the *right* of the center. The server's lead foot can be as near to the baseline as possible *without* actually touching it; but if the server does touch this line before the ball leaves his racquet, he has made a "footfault" and he loses that particular serve. For the service into the Backhand court, the server must stand to the *left* of center, and behind the baseline. The Serve *alternates* between the Forehand and Backhand courts of the server's opponent.

The BEST place to stand when serving in a singles match (two players against each other) is as *near to the center* as possible and just to the *right* or *left* of it.

REASON:

- When your ball has been delivered into the diagonally opposite service court, you are already where you want to be strategically, in the center of your court. If you choose to serve into your opponent's Forehand court from a position far to the right of center, he will — if he is smart — return the ball to the extreme left side of the court and you will have a long way to run for it. In fact, you will be totally unable to reach a fast-paced return of Serve to this point.

► BEST POSITION TO RECEIVE

When you are receiving the Serve, the best place for you to stand is behind the very center of the court to which the ball is directed. Draw an imaginary line from your opponent that bisects the service court. Take a position on this line as deep in the court as you wish, and you will probably have to take only one step to cover a ball directed either to your extreme right or extreme left. This will take care of your position left to right.

The *depth* at which you should stand to *best receive* a Serve is entirely dependent on the speed of your opponent's Serve. If it is fast, you will have a better chance of returning it if you stand deep in the court; if slow, stand closer to the net. In short, after judging the speed of your opponent's Serve (you can get an idea when you are warming up), stand in as close as you dare to the service line, allowing yourself just time to turn and stroke the ball back.

At the beginning of play after each point, you *must* serve into the opposite service court from the one into which you served the last point.

You ALWAYS begin a new *game* by directing your service into the opponent's Forehand service court. After that point is played, the next service goes into his Backhand service court, alternating in this way throughout each *game*.

After each game, the Serve passes to the other side. That is, if you are playing singles, after one of you has served a game, it is the other's turn to serve the next one.

► SERVICE

Each server is allowed two balls. At the beginning of each point, as you get ready to serve, you are obligated to be sure that your opponent is ready to receive. It is customary for the server to say "Ready?" or to hold up the two balls to be served. Upon receiving some acknowledgment from your opponent, such as "I'm ready," or a wave of his racquet, or a nod, then you serve your first ball. This routine is not necessary for the second ball — if you miss with the first one. Your first and second balls are considered to be in rhythm and it is up to the receiver to be ready for the second ball.

If the first ball goes into the proper service court, that ball is "alive," and it is played until the point is over — that is, until one of you fails to return it over the net or into the court. If your first ball fails to go in the proper service court, you are allowed a second ball. If it goes in, you play it. If neither ball goes into the proper service court, you have committed a "double fault" (a Serve that fails to go in is called a "fault"), and the point goes to your opponent.

The only function of the service court is to establish whether the ball is "alive." After it has landed in the proper service court, it may be returned to ANY point within the court, except in the outside alleys that are used only for Doubles play (see court diagram).

► SCORING THE GAME

The game of tennis consists of POINTS, GAMES, and SETS.

Points

After the ball becomes "alive," the contest is to see who can keep it going back over the net and into the opponent's court the greatest number of times. If a ball you have stroked goes outside the limits of the court, or into the net, your opponent wins the point; and vice versa. An "alive" ball must be stroked before it bounces a second time.

You can win a tennis *game* by winning four *points*, PROVIDED that at that time you are ahead of your opponent by at least *two* points. The same requirement holds for the winning of a set. You can win the set by winning *six games,* but you MUST be *two games ahead* at the end of the set.

What happens in a game if, after winning four points, you are NOT two points ahead? You keep playing until *you* are or *he* is.

Each of the game points has a name or a number, and the *server's* score is *always* given *first*. The scoring is as follows:

Zero points — "Love" (Love meaning "zero," or "goose egg," from the French "*l'oeuf*" or egg);

First point — 15;

Second point — 30;

Third point — 40;

WHY 15 for the first point won, 30 for the second, and 40 for the third? There is neither rhyme nor reason to this terminology which is, however, sanctified by tradition, and I advise you not to question it.

Let's take a hypothetical game. You (the server) have won the first point, so the score is "15-Love." You also win the second point, so the score is "30-Love." (Remember, the score of the server is *always* given first.) But I win the next point. You still have 30 but I now have 15, so the score is "30-15." You win the next point; score is "40-15." IF you win the next point — your fourth — you win the game. BUT, if I win the next two points, we arrive at a score of "40-40," and we call this "DEUCE."

Games

Now, one of us must win *two points in a row* to win the game. If you (the server) win the next point, the score is "Advantage In," or "Ad In," as it is called. If you win the point *after* that, it is your game. If, I, your opponent (the receiver), had won the point after "deuce," the score would be "Advantage Out," or "Ad Out," and if I win the next point the game is mine — I took "advantage" of my "advantage."

However, should you (the server) *lose* the next point after the score is "Ad In," the score then comes back to "deuce," or even, and you are at least two points away from winning the game. Remember, after "deuce" (or 40-40) one of us must be able to take *two points in a row* to win the game.

Sets

Now, what if you have won six games but you are not ahead by two? In other words, I have won five, while you have won six. As in the game, so in the set. You can win a set by a score of 6-Love, 6-1, 6-2, 6-3, or 6-4, but NOT 6-5. From this point on the scores for *games* will have to be 7-5, 6-8, 7-9, and so forth. This too, can go, and has, gone on for hours. There is an end, however, to the DEUCE business. You may be relieved to hear that you need only lead by one set to win a match (at least two sets).

REASONS FOR THIS SCORING:

- Why this two-point- and two-game-lead requirement? It was obviously the intention of the designers of the game of tennis to *emphasize* the element of *skill* and to *minimize* the chance of *luck*.

In general, the better player will win every time. This is true in part because of the great number of points played in a match. Every time a ball is served into the opposite court there is a new point. An isolated bad call by an umpire or opponent is minimized in its importance to the match by the very number of points which make it up, as is a freak lucky shot. If one player has clearly demonstrated his superiority in a particular game by going at least two points ahead when he has won four, it is his game. But if the other contestant is within one point of being even, the designers of the game required that the winner clearly establish his superiority by winning two points in a row before he can win the game. The same principle holds true with the set. If the leader is not separated by at least two games from his opponent's score, he must demonstrate his superiority by pulling ahead by two games.

You will remember that luck does enter into the question of who serves first and who plays in which court, but even this luck is minimized. It is customary to change courts after every "odd" game; that is, after the first, third, fifth, etc., games. This eliminates the possibility that one player might have the sun in his eyes during the whole match and thus lose it in spite of superior skill.

► DOUBLES PLAY

We have assumed up to this point that only two people were playing. Suppose that there are four. This is when the rules for "Doubles" take over.

Position in Doubles

The best strategical position from which to serve in doubles is one-half way between the center of the court and the extreme outside line of the court.

REASON:

- This puts you in the exact middle of the court area for which *you* are responsible. Your partner, who is probably standing at the net directly facing the diagonal service court, is responsible for the entire half of the court in which *he* is standing. He is even expected to cope with an effort to lob over his head.

When your partner is serving into your opponents' Forehand service court, if you choose to take the net position, locate yourself exactly the distance of your extended left arm and racquet into the court (toward center of tennis court) from the singles court line and back from the net so that you can just see the service line over the top of the net.

REASON:

- From here in one step you can cover the entire alley and you are as far into the court as you dare to be to help your partner cover the rest of the court. Your distance back from the net helps guard against a lob over your head. Your Ready position at the net is that given for the Overhead Smash and the Volley.

When your partner is serving into the opponents' Backhand service court, use your right hand and racquet to determine the distance you should be into the court from the singles court line.

Alternation in Doubles

In doubles play, as in singles, first one side serves a game and then the other. In addition, the service alternates between the partners on the same side. If A and B are playing against C and D, the service would go A-C-B-D. However, at the beginning of each *new* set, each team can decide on whom they wish to begin serving in the new set. (If in doubt about this or other minor rules of the game, get hold of a USLTA rule book and no one can argue with you).

► THE UNWRITTEN RULES

One of the charms of tennis is its emphasis on fairness and consideration for the other players. For instance, in friendly (non-tournament) play, it is customary, if you for some reason have disturbed the rhythm of your opponent's two serves, to say "Take two," offering him the entire Serve sequence again. This is justified if you have returned the first Serve, discovering too late that it was going to be out of bounds, and thus pulling the server out of position.

There is need for only one word from you about the Serve. The word is "Out." Do not call "Good," and play it back. If you play it back and do *not* say "Out," the Serve IS good. Unnecessary conversation may be disturbing to your opponent and it is an unfair distraction on your part.

Tennis is a highly competitive game, but is one in which it serves no purpose to win unfairly, and this respect for fair if fierce competition is characteristic of tennis wherever it is played around the world.

In a non-tournament game where you must dispense with the services of an umpire, you are the judge of balls falling in your own court. Judge each ball quickly and without regard for whether you need the point or not. If you are in doubt, give your opponent the benefit of the doubt. If you have made a judgment, stick to it. I do not believe that you will lose matches by this method, and you will certainly find your relationship with other players happy. It goes without saying that you will grant your opponent the right to judge the balls on his side and will not argue even if you "know that ball was *in*." These things even themselves up if you yourself follow the unwritten rules of courtesy and fairness.

In a tournament, it is permissible to ask for a disinterested umpire and this is by far the most satisfactory way to play a match.

You now have a good skeletal outline of strokes and rules on which to hang your game of tennis. It is not the purpose of this book to completely flesh out this skeleton. There is material for a whole shelf of books on this wonderful game. However, there are a few points of basic strategy so continuously applicable that I want to re-emphasize them at this point.

▶ BASIC STRATEGY

Basic strategy in tennis has to do in great part with your position in the court at a given time. Should you go to the net or stay back; attack or defend? In short, *where* will you be most effective? The most helpful point I can give you about this is, "ALWAYS CENTER YOURSELF." Leave an even amount of space to your left and to your right. If you are drawn to your right to make a Forehand return, don't stop to admire it. Get back immediately to the center of the court. The return shot, if your opponent is on his toes, will bring the ball far over to your left.

This interval between the time you stroke the ball and it returns to you is the most important time in tennis, and is also the most commonly misused, or not used at all. In many cases its use or misuse differentiates a good player from a poor one. The failure to make use of *this* time results from an impression that, somehow, the ball will "sit" for you, which it will NOT. Between the time when you swing at a ball and the time when the racquet face actually meets it, the ball will have moved considerably.

You must reckon with this motion. To become adept at tennis, you must recognize the fact that tennis is a game of *movement*. Then the BEATS of the stroke, the PREPARATORY movements of the body, and the use of time fall logically into place and make for a realistic and sensible approach to the game. Furthermore, the *use* of this particular time is the only way the strokes given you in this book can be utilized. Avoid flat-footed waiting; dance on your toes; move *before* you think you have to move.

In other words, if you have a FOUR-BEAT movement to perform and only have time for THREE BEATS, then the correct movement is not possible and you are always under muscular strain, which is what we are trying to avoid. At this point, you may well say, as I did early in my career, "But how do I know on which side to start my movement until I see where the ball is going?" The answer I was given I will pass on to you. It is: "ANTICIPATE!" Try it! Start your movement *before* you think you know where the ball is going. In an unbelievably high percentage of the time you will find that you have started right. Very likely in the heat of play our eyes record and mind subconsciously analyzes factors not registered by the conscious mind.

I want to give you here three suggestions that will aid you to be ready:

1. Center yourself as to open spaces your opponent might hit, *before* he strokes the ball. Gain this place by using the time while your ball is traveling into his court.

2. Start your BEAT movements early enough to allow time for a continuous flowing body movement.

3. Time your beginning BEATS on the ground strokes (Forehand and Backhand) so that you have completed your ONE, TWO, and are on the *end* of THREE BEAT by the time the ball *strikes the ground* in front of you.

Before I leave the *basics,* I want to give you one bit of psychology that will stand you in good stead: *always play the COMING point.* You cannot afford to have your mind tied up in what you did wrong on the last point (or points), nor on how far behind you are as a result. No match is lost till the last point is played. Many a victory has been snatched from what seemed like certain defeat by a player who had only *one* thing on his mind — to win the NEXT point.

▶ PROBABILITIES

This is an area where tennis and chess meet. In order to make "ready" for a shot from your opponent, consider what he *can* and *probably will* do. You will find this a most helpful perspective from which to improve your game.

Let's say, for instance, that you have stroked the ball to your opponent's backhand corner. You have come in and taken your Ready position at the net. Your opponent now has only three maneuvers with which he can logically win the point from you:

1. He can try to pass you down the line on your right side (likely). Therefore, you will logically stand slightly nearer the right side of the court.

2. He could put his return ball to your left (unlikely). It is unlikely because he is so far to the left side of the court that the angle his ball must take to avoid you at the net makes it an almost impossible shot.

3. He can go over your head with a lob (likely). You have prepared yourself for this by taking a position 12 to 14 feet back from the net, so as to discourage this shot if possible, and to cover it if it *is* made.

Remember, these are *all* the things your opponent can logically do. He cannot win the point by hitting the ball under the net, nor can he hit it through you. So from your own analysis of what he *can* do, you arrive at a good idea of what he probably *will* do.

Another example: You are playing doubles and you are at the net. You notice that your opponent has a fine, grooved, diagonal return of your partner's Serve, which passes out of reach to your right. He has done this many times without your being able to block the ball. Now, isn't it probable that after such success with this maneuver he will repeat it? Figuring the probabilities, you decide to use your time properly and to arrive simultaneously with the ball at the point where it has been passing over the net. You do and easily volley it away to win the point.

The next time your opponent receives your partner's Serve, it is very likely that he will be suddenly concerned with you and how to avoid you. Since you were successful in cutting off his diagonal return with a Volley last time, he reasons, it is probable that you will do it again. Therefore, he will logically try to pass you down your alley, which you must have left to cut off his ball down the middle.

Figuring these probabilities, this time you feint toward the middle of the court as your opponent is beginning his service return stroke. Then you move quickly back for an easy put-away Volley. *Now* what will this opponent be thinking as he prepares to receive the next Serve? You consider all the probabilities, including the present attitude plus the personality of your opponent. If you have reasoned correctly, you will be ready and waiting at the perfect spot for his next return or Serve. You may also have upset him sufficiently so that this time he will knock the ball completely out of the court.

These are just small illustrations of a certain slant on the whole game, which can be most diverting to you once you have somewhat mastered the technique of your strokes. It is interesting, like chess, and constitutes a veritable game within a game. I thoroughly recommend it to you.

And now, for the rest of your glorious, long and healthy life

PLAY TENNIS!

Towards Excellence

Subtleties for the Advanced

Variety is an element in all superb skills, something that grows out of the original technique. This holds true in painting, music, writing — in short, the Arts — and also in games of pure skill such as chess. Tennis follows the same pattern. A "set" or unvarying game, no matter how severe or how consistent, can be easily understood by your opponent, and therefore countered. The furthest development of a tennis game lies in the variety — without essentially changing the strokes — that skill and imagination can give it.

If you are already an advanced player, you may be at a loss to know how to improve your game any further. In such a case, you should concentrate on the following three areas of your game:

1. Change of pace;

2. Variety in the Serve; and

3. Taking (stroking) the ball at different places in its bounce.

► CHANGE OF PACE (SPEED)

Change of pace is used to counter the rhythm of an opponent. If his rhythm is allowed to dominate the game, you lose. *Disguise* and *variety* are the special elements in the change-of-pace skill.

To change pace, *increase* or *decrease* the length and speed of the pattern beats of the stroke, with emphasis on the last beat.

The change of pace must be executed on the same unvarying beat pattern of the stroke, so that an opponent cannot read from the movements that there will be a change of speed on the ball.

DO NOT ELIMINATE A STROKE BEAT FOR A CHANGE OF PACE!

Go through the turn and the beat pattern on a smaller or larger scale, or with a faster or slower movement. Do this even to stroke a very easy slow ball. This will serve to establish and hold the beat pattern of the stroke. Even *one* compromise with the beat pattern of the stroke can do much damage. Strokes are the *tools* when playing tennis, and they must be kept polished and intact.

▶ SERVE VARIETY

All players fall into a set pattern of Serve motions. Once the Serve windup starts, there follows an unchanging body-movement sequence. But from this same delivery pattern the spin, pace, bounce, and direction of the served ball can be changed. The ability to do this gives the Serve its variety.

The three basic Serves (spin variations) are struck in the following relationship to the server on the Serve arc:

The FLAT Serve spins scarcely at all:

 (Has medium-height bounce. Hard Serve.)

The pure SLICE spins from left to right:

 (Low bounce; jumps to side; speed subtracted by spin.)

The pure TWIST spins from bottom to top:

 (High bounce; jumps to side; power and speed subtracted by spin.)

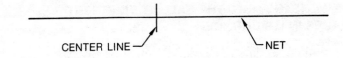

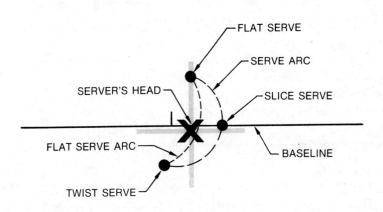

The "big" Serve is a mixture of all three of these. The infinite variety of the Serve lies in the combination of these basic spins. The chosen mixture is best achieved by first contacting the ball at *different places* on the Serve arc. Experimenting with this Serve arc will show that the bounce of the served ball can vary (depending on the mixture of spins) from extremely high bounces (5 to 8 feet), to low bounces scarcely rising from the court. Pace can vary from fast to slow from the same Serve motion.

The ability to change the spin on the ball is a useful Serve weapon, and if possessed will allow the server to counter his opponent's ability to "get set" for a certain delivery. As one grows older, he will find this to be a skill that will enable him to compete with younger and more agile players. You can compare this to the old baseball pitcher who baffles the batter with the "stuff" on his "nothing" ball. But more to the point, the science, skill, and lasting joy in tennis lie in exploring the truly infinite variations that can be applied to the ball.

DO NOT CHANGE THE BEAT PATTERN
TO VARY THE SERVE!

► TAKING (STROKING) THE BALL AT DIFFERENT PLACES IN ITS BOUNCE

This skill comes late in the development of a player and involves one of the most subtle and delicate skills. It is used in handling ground strokes (Forehand and Backhand).

A tennis ball hits the court surface, rises in a small arc at the top of its bounce and then begins to drop:

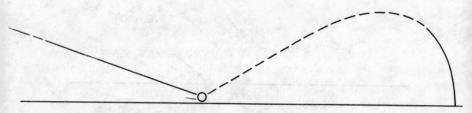

The grips you have learned are designed to stroke the ball *before* it starts its descent from the small arc. Begin experimenting with taking the ball at different places along the dotted line in the illustration above. Exact computations have not been made, but 2 inches forward (sooner) on taking the bounce will take many steps away from an opponent. For instance, if you are hitting ground strokes from corner to corner, and you begin working this subtle skill of taking the ball further and further forward in its bounce, it is possible to have an opponent at one side of the court while your stroked ball is settling in the other corner. Imagine the power of this skill! As far as your opponent can see, you are stroking the ball at the same power each time, yet somehow he seems to be further and further behind on reaching the ball until he finally cannot put his racquet on it.

This has the same effect as change of pace, but utilizes a different means. Again, always make the same BEAT PATTERN of your stroke. If you are handling a very fast ball, simply narrow the area of your beat. Make the complete beat pattern in a smaller area.

Tips for the Coach

The following tips are based not only on my own experience as a coach, but are also the result of attendance at literally hundreds of meets where I watched coaches with their teams, and picked up further pointers on what to do and not do.

► EXERCISES AND PRACTICE

In general, devise practice methods which use the muscles and qualities demanded by the game.

1. Demand stamina; it is essential to the game. Develop this by regular running exercises BUT

- Have the players run around the courts backwards
- Have them run sideways
- Have the players run backwards and sideways against time
- Combine a continuous jog with short dashes. Devise a mile or two run interspersed throughout with all-out dashes.

2. Have four players rally — groundstroke — back and forth across the net, each pair keeping the ball in the same alley. At a signal, have the players cross the balls to the opposite alley.

3. In Volley practice, put two players against one at the net.

4. In Overhead Smash practice, assign half the team to toss balls into the air, and the other half to bring them down. Then shift, making the hitters throw.

- Devise a game where the "Overhead Smasher" may continue smashing balls until he misses; then have the thrower replace him.

5. Practice drop-shots by a game in which the service line becomes the outer border of the court. Have a player serve a drop-shot into the opposite service court. The opposing player returns a drop-shot any place within the two service courts, and so on until one misses. Make the game a certain number of points — such as 10.

6. Have a set amount of Serve practice each day.

Whatever you do, try to get a variety of Serve delivery into your players' bags of skills. Impress upon them that change of pace is one of the great tennis weapons. Show them the infinite variety of spins which may be given a ball. In this connection, have them read carefully the preceding chapter, "Subtleties for the Advanced," and work with them on developing the skills described there. Allow whole periods of time for experimentation on varieties of spin delivery. During these periods, do not reward or count accuracy.

► TEAM SELECTION

Make your team selection on a mathematical basis of matches won or lost against teammates. Start these matches early in the year. Set up a fair match-challenge procedure — that is, a match not played within one week of a challenge is defaulted.

► COACHING THE ADVANCED PLAYER

You will likely find on your team an outstanding player; one who has moved beyond the surrounding competition. This player will seem so far advanced that you may be at a loss as to how best to help him or her improve still further. Now is when you should have this player concentrate on the following three areas of his game:

(1) Change of pace;

(2) Variety in the Serve; and

(3) Taking (stroking) the ball at different places in its bounce.

These three are discussed, explained, and illustrated in the preceding chapter, "Subtleties for the Advanced." Each section of this chapter should be read carefully by the student and the techniques involved gone over in detail — preferably with the coach — before he begins practice on any part of it.

► MECHANICAL AIDS

The best pick-me-up I know is to have a *damp* cloth with which the player can towel his face and the back of his neck. Have this ready when your players change courts. Naturally, the standard dry towel should be available also.

Have your players rinse out their mouths with water. Advise them not to drink deeply; let the fewest possible drops go down.

Have salt tablets available to counter exhaustion.

► WHEN YOU ARE HOST FOR A MATCH

Go out of your way to be accommodating to visiting players, because this is traditional in tennis. If possible, arrange some special treat for them. Have water at the court, towels (both dry and damp), and remember that it is up to you to furnish the balls.

► THE GAME — STRATEGY

During a match do not offer advice from the sidelines; it is not expected of you.

Tell your players to go into each match with a mapped-out strategy for victory. If the opponent is an unknown quantity, your player must map his strategy during the warmup period. Tell him to note carefully how his opponent hits each stroke and how he moves. Any observed weakness can become the basis of a winning strategy. Play the weakness. Has the opponent *one* stroke that he does not handle well? Play it. Does he move slowly or badly? Then make him run.

During the match your players:

1. Should give each pre-decided strategem full chance to develop — perhaps for as long as a full set.

2. Should NOT change a winning game.

3. Should CHANGE a losing game.

4. When winning, should move the game along as quickly as possible. Do not be turned aside.

5. When losing, should slow the game as much as possible within legal limits. Be deliberate. (When losing, your player has been caught up in his opponent's rhythm and pace. He must change the pace and in that way break the rhythm.)

6. Should change the pace by taking the ball sooner, or later, in its bounce. OR if the balls have been coming hard and low, should lift their balls back high. If the balls have been coming high and slow, they should hit their returns low and hard.

7. Should experiment with their games when losing; when winning, DO NOT experiment.

▶ TIPS ON DOUBLES STRATEGY

Doubles, even more than singles, is a game of strategy, and all the tips on singles also apply to it.

1. Caution your players *not* to criticize one another *during* a match. Analyze, huddle, make decisions, but do *not* criticize personally.

2. A player should encourage his partner throughout the match. At every good shot the partner makes, say "Great!" He should *ignore* all the bad shots. This will pay off and will more often than not bring the partner out of a slump. If one of the partners can't refrain from criticizing every time he speaks, he should keep his mouth *shut*.

3. Tell the net player to be a factor in the game. Tell him to "poach" — steal the ball — occasionally. Even if he loses the point, he will be a hazard in the minds of the opponents. He must *not* present a stationary, never-changing picture to them.

4. In some cases, the server can come in too fast. If he cannot get in soon enough to make a *good* volley, he would be wise to come in more slowly and make the *second* shot a good volley.

In every case, the server must design to join his partner at the net or he will isolate him there.

5. In doubles, if a player is not moving or about to move to another position, he is strategically wrong. If one player leaves an opening on the court to make a shot, his partner should cover it.

6. The best overall strategy in doubles is to present a constant horizontal line to the opponents — that is, partners abreast facing the net. If one partner goes back to cover a lob, the other partner should cross to the side he has left and arrive parallel with him as he returns the lob.

7. If there is *any* doubt as to the direction in which a player wishes a volley to go, he should hit it down the middle between the two opponents. This is the safest shot to make and will probably afford another shot at the ball.

► AFTER THE MATCH

Tennis is an emotional game. When dealing with emotion, exercise careful judgment. Encouragement, in general, is better than adverse criticism.

Analysis of the history of a match should be kept in abstract, logical, non-personal terms.

Demand that a player learn *something* from every match he plays:

1. Before a match state, "I expect you to do your best. Whether you win or lose, I will want you to bring me one piece of knowledge you gain from playing this match."

2. Be satisfied with, "He certainly can bring his Backhand down my Forehand line."

3. Do not be satisfied with the general, "Well, he's better than I am." *Why* is he better?

ANALYZE, EXPERIMENT, CHANGE.
BUT NEVER, NEVER GIVE UP!

A PERSONAL WORD FROM MELVIN POWERS
PUBLISHER, WILSHIRE BOOK COMPANY

Dear Friend:

My goal is to publish interesting, informative, and inspirational books. You can help me accomplish this by answering the following questions, either by phone or by mail. Or, if convenient for you, I would welcome the opportunity to visit with you in my office and hear your comments in person.

Did you enjoy reading this book? Why?

Would you enjoy reading another similar book?

What idea in the book impressed you the most?

If applicable to your situation, have you incorporated this idea in your daily life?

Is there a chapter that could serve as a theme for an entire book? Please explain.

If you have an idea for a book, I would welcome discussing it with you. If you already have one in progress, write or call me concerning possible publication. I can be reached at (213) 875-1711 or (213) 983-1105.

Sincerely yours,

MELVIN POWERS

12015 Sherman Road
North Hollywood, California 91605

MELVIN POWERS SELF-IMPROVEMENT LIBRARY

ASTROLOGY

———ASTROLOGY: A FASCINATING HISTORY *P. Naylor*	2.00
———ASTROLOGY: HOW TO CHART YOUR HOROSCOPE *Max Heindel*	3.00
———ASTROLOGY: YOUR PERSONAL SUN-SIGN GUIDE *Beatrice Ryder*	3.00
———ASTROLOGY FOR EVERYDAY LIVING *Janet Harris*	2.00
———ASTROLOGY MADE EASY *Astarte*	2.00
———ASTROLOGY MADE PRACTICAL *Alexandra Kayhle*	3.00
———ASTROLOGY, ROMANCE, YOU AND THE STARS *Anthony Norvell*	4.00
———MY WORLD OF ASTROLOGY *Sydney Omarr*	4.00
———THOUGHT DIAL *Sydney Omarr*	3.00
———ZODIAC REVEALED *Rupert Gleadow*	2.00

BRIDGE

———BRIDGE BIDDING MADE EASY *Edwin B. Kantar*	5.00
———BRIDGE CONVENTIONS *Edwin B. Kantar*	4.00
———BRIDGE HUMOR *Edwin B. Kantar*	3.00
———COMPETITIVE BIDDING IN MODERN BRIDGE *Edgar Kaplan*	4.00
———DEFENSIVE BRIDGE PLAY COMPLETE *Edwin B. Kantar*	10.00
———HOW TO IMPROVE YOUR BRIDGE *Alfred Sheinwold*	2.00
———INTRODUCTION TO DEFENDER'S PLAY *Edwin B. Kantar*	3.00
———TEST YOUR BRIDGE PLAY *Edwin B. Kantar*	3.00
———WINNING DECLARER PLAY *Dorothy Hayden Truscott*	4.00

BUSINESS, STUDY & REFERENCE

———CONVERSATION MADE EASY *Elliot Russell*	2.00
———EXAM SECRET *Dennis B. Jackson*	2.00
———FIX-IT BOOK *Arthur Symons*	2.00
———HOW TO DEVELOP A BETTER SPEAKING VOICE *M. Hellier*	2.00
———HOW TO MAKE A FORTUNE IN REAL ESTATE *Albert Winnikoff*	3.00
———INCREASE YOUR LEARNING POWER *Geoffrey A. Dudley*	2.00
———MAGIC OF NUMBERS *Robert Tocquet*	2.00
———PRACTICAL GUIDE TO BETTER CONCENTRATION *Melvin Powers*	2.00
———PRACTICAL GUIDE TO PUBLIC SPEAKING *Maurice Forley*	3.00
———7 DAYS TO FASTER READING *William S. Schaill*	2.00
———SONGWRITERS RHYMING DICTIONARY *Jane Shaw Whitfield*	5.00
———SPELLING MADE EASY *Lester D. Basch & Dr. Milton Finkelstein*	2.00
———STUDENT'S GUIDE TO BETTER GRADES *J. A. Rickard*	2.00
———TEST YOURSELF—Find Your Hidden Talent *Jack Shafer*	2.00
———YOUR WILL & WHAT TO DO ABOUT IT *Attorney Samuel G. Kling*	3.00

CALLIGRAPHY

———CALLIGRAPHY—The Art of Beautfiul Writing *Katherine Jeffares*	5.00

CHESS & CHECKERS

———BEGINNER'S GUIDE TO WINNING CHESS *Fred Reinfeld*	3.00
———BETTER CHESS—How to Play *Fred Reinfeld*	2.00
———CHECKERS MADE EASY *Tom Wiswell*	2.00
———CHESS IN TEN EASY LESSONS *Larry Evans*	2.00
———CHESS MADE EASY *Milton L. Hanauer*	2.00
———CHESS MASTERY—A New Approach *Fred Reinfeld*	2.00
———CHESS PROBLEMS FOR BEGINNERS *edited by Fred Reinfeld*	2.00
———CHESS SECRETS REVEALED *Fred Reinfeld*	2.00
———CHESS STRATEGY—An Expert's Guide *Fred Reinfeld*	2.00
———CHESS TACTICS FOR BEGINNERS *edited by Fred Reinfeld*	2.00
———CHESS THEORY & PRACTICE *Morry & Mitchell*	2.00
———HOW TO WIN AT CHECKERS *Fred Reinfeld*	2.00
———1001 BRILLIANT WAYS TO CHECKMATE *Fred Reinfeld*	3.00
———1001 WINNING CHESS SACRIFICES & COMBINATIONS *Fred Reinfeld*	3.00
———SOVIET CHESS *Edited by R. G. Wade*	3.00

COOKERY & HERBS

———CULPEPER'S HERBAL REMEDIES *Dr. Nicholas Culpeper*	2.00
———FAST GOURMET COOKBOOK *Poppy Cannon*	2.50

_____HEALING POWER OF HERBS *May Bethel*	3.00
_____HERB HANDBOOK *Dawn MacLeod*	2.00
_____HERBS FOR COOKING AND HEALING *Dr. Donald Law*	2.00
_____HERBS FOR HEALTH—How to Grow & Use Them *Louise Evans Doole*	2.00
_____HOME GARDEN COOKBOOK—Delicious Natural Food Recipes *Ken Kraft*	3.00
_____MEDICAL HERBALIST *edited by Dr. J. R. Yemm*	3.00
_____NATURAL FOOD COOKBOOK *Dr. Harry C. Bond*	3.00
_____NATURE'S MEDICINES *Richard Lucas*	3.00
_____VEGETABLE GARDENING FOR BEGINNERS *Hugh Wiberg*	2.00
_____VEGETABLES FOR TODAY'S GARDENS *R. Milton Carleton*	2.00
_____VEGETARIAN COOKERY *Janet Walker*	3.00
_____VEGETARIAN COOKING MADE EASY & DELECTABLE *Veronica Vezza*	2.00
_____VEGETARIAN DELIGHTS—A Happy Cookbook for Health *K. R. Mehta*	2.00
_____VEGETARIAN GOURMET COOKBOOK *Joyce McKinnel*	2.00

GAMBLING & POKER

_____ADVANCED POKER STRATEGY & WINNING PLAY *A. D. Livingston*	3.00
_____HOW NOT TO LOSE AT POKER *Jeffrey Lloyd Castle*	3.00
_____HOW TO WIN AT DICE GAMES *Skip Frey*	3.00
_____HOW TO WIN AT POKER *Terence Reese & Anthony T. Watkins*	2.00
_____SECRETS OF WINNING POKER *George S. Coffin*	3.00
_____WINNING AT CRAPS *Dr. Lloyd T. Commins*	2.00
_____WINNING AT GIN *Chester Wander & Cy Rice*	3.00
_____WINNING AT 21—An Expert's Guide *John Archer*	3.00
_____WINNING POKER SYSTEMS *Norman Zadeh*	3.00

HEALTH

_____DR. LINDNER'S SPECIAL WEIGHT CONTROL METHOD	1.50
_____HELP YOURSELF TO BETTER SIGHT *Margaret Darst Corbett*	3.00
_____HOW TO IMPROVE YOUR VISION *Dr. Robert A. Kraskin*	2.00
_____HOW YOU CAN STOP SMOKING PERMANENTLY *Ernest Caldwell*	2.00
_____MIND OVER PLATTER *Peter G. Lindner, M.D.*	2.00
_____NATURE'S WAY TO NUTRITION & VIBRANT HEALTH *Robert J. Scrutton*	3.00
_____NEW CARBOHYDRATE DIET COUNTER *Patti Lopez-Pereira*	1.50
_____PSYCHEDELIC ECSTASY *William Marshall & Gilbert W. Taylor*	2.00
_____REFLEXOLOGY *Dr. Maybelle Segal*	2.00
_____YOU CAN LEARN TO RELAX *Dr. Samuel Gutwirth*	2.00
_____YOUR ALLERGY—What To Do About It *Allan Knight, M.D.*	2.00

HOBBIES

_____BATON TWIRLING—A Complete Illustrated Guide *Doris Wheelus*	4.00
_____BEACHCOMBING FOR BEGINNERS *Norman Hickin*	2.00
_____BLACKSTONE'S MODERN CARD TRICKS *Harry Blackstone*	2.00
_____BLACKSTONE'S SECRETS OF MAGIC *Harry Blackstone*	2.00
_____BUTTERFLIES	2.50
_____COIN COLLECTING FOR BEGINNERS *Burton Hobson & Fred Reinfeld*	2.00
_____ENTERTAINING WITH ESP *Tony 'Doc' Shiels*	2.00
_____400 FASCINATING MAGIC TRICKS YOU CAN DO *Howard Thurston*	3.00
_____GOULD'S GOLD & SILVER GUIDE TO COINS *Maurice Gould*	2.00
_____HOW I TURN JUNK INTO FUN AND PROFIT *Sari*	3.00
_____HOW TO PLAY THE HARMONICA FOR FUN AND PROFIT *Hal Leighton*	3.00
_____HOW TO WRITE A HIT SONG & SELL IT *Tommy Boyce*	7.00
_____JUGGLING MADE EASY *Rudolf Dittrich*	2.00
_____MAGIC MADE EASY *Byron Wels*	2.00
_____SEW SIMPLY, SEW RIGHT *Mini Rhea & F. Leighton*	2.00
_____STAMP COLLECTING FOR BEGINNERS *Burton Hobson*	2.00
_____STAMP COLLECTING FOR FUN & PROFIT *Frank Cetin*	2.00

HORSE PLAYERS' WINNING GUIDES

_____BETTING HORSES TO WIN *Les Conklin*	3.00
_____ELIMINATE THE LOSERS *Bob McKnight*	3.00
_____HOW TO PICK WINNING HORSES *Bob McKnight*	3.00
_____HOW TO WIN AT THE RACES *Sam (The Genius) Lewin*	3.00
_____HOW YOU CAN BEAT THE RACES *Jack Kavanagh*	3.00

———MAKING MONEY AT THE RACES *David Barr*	3.00
———PAYDAY AT THE RACES *Les Conklin*	2.00
———SMART HANDICAPPING MADE EASY *William Bauman*	3.00
———SUCCESS AT THE HARNESS RACES *Barry Meadow*	2.50
———WINNING AT THE HARNESS RACES—An Expert's Guide *Nick Cammarano*	2.50

HUMOR

———HOW TO BE A COMEDIAN FOR FUN & PROFIT *King & Laufer*	2.00
———JOKE TELLER'S HANDBOOK *Bob Orben*	3.00

HYPNOTISM

———ADVANCED TECHNIQUES OF HYPNOSIS *Melvin Powers*	2.00
———BRAINWASHING AND THE CULTS *Paul A. Verdier, Ph.D.*	3.00
———CHILDBIRTH WITH HYPNOSIS *William S. Kroger, M.D.*	3.00
———HOW TO SOLVE Your Sex Problems with Self-Hypnosis *Frank S. Caprio, M.D.*	2.00
———HOW TO STOP SMOKING THRU SELF-HYPNOSIS *Leslie M. LeCron*	2.00
———HOW TO USE AUTO-SUGGESTION EFFECTIVELY *John Duckworth*	2.00
———HOW YOU CAN BOWL BETTER USING SELF-HYPNOSIS *Jack Heise*	2.00
———HOW YOU CAN PLAY BETTER GOLF USING SELF-HYPNOSIS *Jack Heise*	2.00
———HYPNOSIS AND SELF-HYPNOSIS *Bernard Hollander, M.D.*	3.00
———HYPNOTISM *(Originally published in 1893)* *Carl Sextus*	3.00
———HYPNOTISM & PSYCHIC PHENOMENA *Simeon Edmunds*	3.00
———HYPNOTISM MADE EASY *Dr. Ralph Winn*	3.00
———HYPNOTISM MADE PRACTICAL *Louis Orton*	2.00
———HYPNOTISM REVEALED *Melvin Powers*	2.00
———HYPNOTISM TODAY *Leslie LeCron and Jean Bordeaux, Ph.D.*	4.00
———MODERN HYPNOSIS *Lesley Kuhn & Salvatore Russo, Ph.D.*	4.00
———NEW CONCEPTS OF HYPNOSIS *Bernard C. Gindes, M.D.*	4.00
———NEW SELF-HYPNOSIS *Paul Adams*	3.00
———POST-HYPNOTIC INSTRUCTIONS—Suggestions for Therapy *Arnold Furst*	3.00
———PRACTICAL GUIDE TO SELF-HYPNOSIS *Melvin Powers*	2.00
———PRACTICAL HYPNOTISM *Philip Magonet, M.D.*	2.00
———SECRETS OF HYPNOTISM *S. J. Van Pelt, M.D.*	3.00
———SELF-HYPNOSIS Its Theory, Technique & Application *Melvin Powers*	2.00
———SELF-HYPNOSIS A Conditioned-Response Technique *Laurance Sparks*	4.00
———THERAPY THROUGH HYPNOSIS *edited by Raphael H. Rhodes*	3.00

JUDAICA

———HOW TO LIVE A RICHER & FULLER LIFE *Rabbi Edgar F. Magnin*	2.00
———MODERN ISRAEL *Lily Edelman*	2.00
———OUR JEWISH HERITAGE *Rabbi Alfred Wolf & Joseph Gaer*	2.00
———ROMANCE OF HASSIDISM *Jacob S. Minkin*	2.50
———SERVICE OF THE HEART *Evelyn Garfiel, Ph.D.*	4.00
———STORY OF ISRAEL IN COINS *Jean & Maurice Gould*	2.00
———STORY OF ISRAEL IN STAMPS *Maxim & Gabriel Shamir*	1.00
———TONGUE OF THE PROPHETS *Robert St. John*	3.00
———TREASURY OF COMFORT *edited by Rabbi Sidney Greenberg*	4.00

JUST FOR WOMEN

———COSMOPOLITAN'S GUIDE TO MARVELOUS MEN Fwd. by *Helen Gurley Brown*	3.00
———COSMOPOLITAN'S NEW ETIQUETTE GUIDE Fwd. by *Helen Gurley Brown*	4.00
———COSMOPOLITAN'S HANG-UP HANDBOOK Foreword by *Helen Gurley Brown*	4.00
———COSMOPOLITAN'S LOVE BOOK—A Guide to Ecstasy in Bed	3.00
———JUST FOR WOMEN—A Guide to the Female Body *Richard E. Sand, M.D.*	3.00
———NEW APPROACHES TO SEX IN MARRIAGE *John E. Eichenlaub, M.D.*	3.00
———SEXUALLY ADEQUATE FEMALE *Frank S. Caprio, M.D.*	2.00
———YOUR FIRST YEAR OF MARRIAGE *Dr. Tom McGinnis*	3.00

MARRIAGE, SEX & PARENTHOOD

———ABILITY TO LOVE *Dr. Allan Fromme*	4.00
———ENCYCLOPEDIA OF MODERN SEX & LOVE TECHNIQUES *Macandrew*	4.00
———GUIDE TO SUCCESSFUL MARRIAGE *Drs. Albert Ellis & Robert Harper*	3.00
———HOW TO RAISE AN EMOTIONALLY HEALTHY, HAPPY CHILD *A. Ellis*	3.00
———IMPOTENCE & FRIGIDITY *Edwin W. Hirsch, M.D.*	3.00
———SEX WITHOUT GUILT *Albert Ellis, Ph.D.*	3.00

_____SEXUALLY ADEQUATE MALE *Frank S. Caprio, M.D.*	3.00

METAPHYSICS & OCCULT

_____BOOK OF TALISMANS, AMULETS & ZODIACAL GEMS *William Pavitt*	4.00
_____CONCENTRATION—A Guide to Mental Mastery *Mouni Sadhu*	3.00
_____CRITIQUES OF GOD *Edited by Peter Angeles*	7.00
_____DREAMS & OMENS REVEALED *Fred Gettings*	2.00
_____EXTRASENSORY PERCEPTION *Simeon Edmunds*	2.00
_____EXTRA-TERRESTRIAL INTELLIGENCE—The First Encounter	6.00
_____FORTUNE TELLING WITH CARDS *P. Foli*	2.00
_____HANDWRITING ANALYSIS MADE EASY *John Marley*	2.00
_____HANDWRITING TELLS *Nadya Olyanova*	3.00
_____HOW TO UNDERSTAND YOUR DREAMS *Geoffrey A. Dudley*	2.00
_____ILLUSTRATED YOGA *William Zorn*	3.00
_____IN DAYS OF GREAT PEACE *Mouni Sadhu*	3.00
_____KING SOLOMON'S TEMPLE IN THE MASONIC TRADITION *Alex Horne*	5.00
_____LSD—THE AGE OF MIND *Bernard Roseman*	2.00
_____MAGICIAN—His training and work *W. E. Butler*	2.00
_____MEDITATION *Mouni Sadhu*	4.00
_____MODERN NUMEROLOGY *Morris C. Goodman*	3.00
_____NUMEROLOGY—ITS FACTS AND SECRETS *Ariel Yvon Taylor*	2.00
_____PALMISTRY MADE EASY *Fred Gettings*	2.00
_____PALMISTRY MADE PRACTICAL *Elizabeth Daniels Squire*	3.00
_____PALMISTRY SECRETS REVEALED *Henry Frith*	2.00
_____PRACTICAL YOGA *Ernest Wood*	3.00
_____PROPHECY IN OUR TIME *Martin Ebon*	2.50
_____PSYCHOLOGY OF HANDWRITING *Nadya Olyanova*	3.00
_____SEEING INTO THE FUTURE *Harvey Day*	2.00
_____SUPERSTITION—Are you superstitious? *Eric Maple*	2.00
_____TAROT *Mouni Sadhu*	4.00
_____TAROT OF THE BOHEMIANS *Papus*	5.00
_____TEST YOUR ESP *Martin Ebon*	2.00
_____WAYS TO SELF-REALIZATION *Mouni Sadhu*	3.00
_____WITCHCRAFT, MAGIC & OCCULTISM—A Fascinating History *W. B. Crow*	3.00
_____WITCHCRAFT—THE SIXTH SENSE *Justine Glass*	2.00
_____WORLD OF PSYCHIC RESEARCH *Hereward Carrington*	2.00
_____YOU CAN ANALYZE HANDWRITING *Robert Holder*	2.00

SELF-HELP & INSPIRATIONAL

_____CYBERNETICS WITHIN US *Y. Saparina*	3.00
_____DAILY POWER FOR JOYFUL LIVING *Dr. Donald Curtis*	2.00
_____DOCTOR PSYCHO-CYBERNETICS *Maxwell Maltz, M.D.*	3.00
_____DYNAMIC THINKING *Melvin Powers*	2.00
_____EXUBERANCE—Your Guide to Happiness & Fulfillment *Dr. Paul Kurtz*	3.00
_____GREATEST POWER IN THE UNIVERSE *U. S. Andersen*	4.00
_____GROW RICH WHILE YOU SLEEP *Ben Sweetland*	3.00
_____GROWTH THROUGH REASON *Albert Ellis, Ph.D.*	3.00
_____GUIDE TO DEVELOPING YOUR POTENTIAL *Herbert A. Otto, Ph.D.*	3.00
_____GUIDE TO LIVING IN BALANCE *Frank S. Caprio, M.D.*	2.00
_____HELPING YOURSELF WITH APPLIED PSYCHOLOGY *R. Henderson*	2.00
_____HELPING YOURSELF WITH PSYCHIATRY *Frank S. Caprio, M.D.*	2.00
_____HOW TO ATTRACT GOOD LUCK *A. H. Z. Carr*	3.00
_____HOW TO CONTROL YOUR DESTINY *Norvell*	3.00
_____HOW TO DEVELOP A WINNING PERSONALITY *Martin Panzer*	3.00
_____HOW TO DEVELOP AN EXCEPTIONAL MEMORY *Young & Gibson*	3.00
_____HOW TO OVERCOME YOUR FEARS *M. P. Leahy, M.D.*	2.00
_____HOW YOU CAN HAVE CONFIDENCE AND POWER *Les Giblin*	3.00
_____HUMAN PROBLEMS & HOW TO SOLVE THEM *Dr. Donald Curtis*	3.00
_____I CAN *Ben Sweetland*	4.00
_____I WILL *Ben Sweetland*	3.00
_____LEFT-HANDED PEOPLE *Michael Barsley*	3.00
_____MAGIC IN YOUR MIND *U. S. Andersen*	3.00

____MAGIC OF THINKING BIG *Dr. David J. Schwartz*	3.00
____MAGIC POWER OF YOUR MIND *Walter M. Germain*	4.00
____MENTAL POWER THROUGH SLEEP SUGGESTION *Melvin Powers*	2.00
____NEW GUIDE TO RATIONAL LIVING *Albert Ellis, Ph.D. & R. Harper, Ph.D.*	3.00
____OUR TROUBLED SELVES *Dr. Allan Fromme*	3.00
____PRACTICAL GUIDE TO SUCCESS & POPULARITY *C. W. Bailey*	2.00
____PSYCHO-CYBERNETICS *Maxwell Maltz, M.D.*	2.00
____SCIENCE OF MIND IN DAILY LIVING *Dr. Donald Curtis*	2.00
____SECRET POWER OF THE PYRAMIDS *U. S. Andersen*	4.00
____SECRET OF SECRETS *U. S. Andersen*	4.00
____STUTTERING AND WHAT YOU CAN DO ABOUT IT *W. Johnson, Ph.D.*	2.50
____SUCCESS-CYBERNETICS *U. S. Andersen*	4.00
____10 DAYS TO A GREAT NEW LIFE *William E. Edwards*	3.00
____THINK AND GROW RICH *Napoleon Hill*	3.00
____THREE MAGIC WORDS *U. S. Andersen*	4.00
____TREASURY OF THE ART OF LIVING *Sidney S. Greenberg*	5.00
____YOU ARE NOT THE TARGET *Laura Huxley*	3.00
____YOUR SUBCONSCIOUS POWER *Charles M. Simmons*	4.00
____YOUR THOUGHTS CAN CHANGE YOUR LIFE *Dr. Donald Curtis*	3.00

SPORTS

____ARCHERY—An Expert's Guide *Dan Stamp*	2.00
____BICYCLING FOR FUN AND GOOD HEALTH *Kenneth E. Luther*	2.00
____BILLIARDS—Pocket • Carom • Three Cushion *Clive Cottingham, Jr.*	2.00
____CAMPING-OUT 101 Ideas & Activities *Bruno Knobel*	2.00
____COMPLETE GUIDE TO FISHING *Vlad Evanoff*	2.00
____HOW TO WIN AT POCKET BILLIARDS *Edward D. Knuchell*	3.00
____LEARNING & TEACHING SOCCER SKILLS *Eric Worthington*	3.00
____MOTORCYCLING FOR BEGINNERS *I. G. Edmonds*	2.00
____PRACTICAL BOATING *W. S. Kals*	3.00
____SECRET OF BOWLING STRIKES *Dawson Taylor*	2.00
____SECRET OF PERFECT PUTTING *Horton Smith & Dawson Taylor*	3.00
____SECRET WHY FISH BITE *James Westman*	2.00
____SKIER'S POCKET BOOK *Otti Wiedman* (4¼″ x 6″)	2.50
____SOCCER—The game & how to play it *Gary Rosenthal*	2.00
____STARTING SOCCER *Edward F. Dolan, Jr.*	2.00
____TABLE TENNIS MADE EASY *Johnny Leach*	2.00

TENNIS LOVERS' LIBRARY

____BEGINNER'S GUIDE TO WINNING TENNIS *Helen Hull Jacobs*	2.00
____HOW TO BEAT BETTER TENNIS PLAYERS *Loring Fiske*	4.00
____HOW TO IMPROVE YOUR TENNIS—Style, Strategy & Analysis *C. Wilson*	2.00
____INSIDE TENNIS—Techniques of Winning *Jim Leighton*	3.00
____PLAY TENNIS WITH ROSEWALL *Ken Rosewall*	2.00
____PSYCH YOURSELF TO BETTER TENNIS *Dr. Walter A. Luszki*	2.00
____SUCCESSFUL TENNIS *Neale Fraser*	2.00
____TENNIS FOR BEGINNERS *Dr. H. A. Murray*	2.00
____TENNIS MADE EASY *Joel Brecheen*	2.00
____WEEKEND TENNIS—How to have fun & win at the same time *Bill Talbert*	3.00
____WINNING WITH PERCENTAGE TENNIS—Smart Strategy *Jack Lowe*	2.00

WILSHIRE PET LIBRARY

____DOG OBEDIENCE TRAINING *Gust Kessopulos*	3.00
____DOG TRAINING MADE EASY & FUN *John W. Kellogg*	2.00
____HOW TO BRING UP YOUR PET DOG *Kurt Unkelbach*	2.00
____HOW TO RAISE & TRAIN YOUR PUPPY *Jeff Griffen*	2.00
____PIGEONS: HOW TO RAISE & TRAIN THEM *William H. Allen, Jr.*	2.00

The books listed above can be obtained from your book dealer or directly from Melvin Powers. When ordering, please remit 25c per book postage & handling. Send for our free illustrated catalog of self-improvement books.

Melvin Powers
12015 Sherman Road, No. Hollywood, California 91605

_____AMATEUR HORSE BREEDER *A. C. Leighton Hardman*	3.00
_____AMERICAN QUARTER HORSE IN PICTURES *Margaret Cabell Self*	3.00
_____APPALOOSA HORSE *Donna & Bill Richardson*	3.00
_____ARABIAN HORSE *Reginald S. Summerhays*	2.00
_____ART OF WESTERN RIDING *Suzanne Norton Jones*	3.00
_____AT THE HORSE SHOW *Margaret Cabell Self*	3.00
_____BACK-YARD FOAL *Peggy Jett Pittinger*	3.00
_____BACK-YARD HORSE *Peggy Jett Pittinger*	3.00
_____BASIC DRESSAGE *Jean Froissard*	2.00
_____BEGINNER'S GUIDE TO HORSEBACK RIDING *Sheila Wall*	2.00
_____BEGINNER'S GUIDE TO THE WESTERN HORSE *Natlee Kenoyer*	2.00
_____BITS—THEIR HISTORY, USE AND MISUSE *Louis Taylor*	3.00
_____BREAKING & TRAINING THE DRIVING HORSE *Doris Ganton*	2.00
_____BREAKING YOUR HORSE'S BAD HABITS *W. Dayton Sumner*	3.00
_____CAVALRY MANUAL OF HORSEMANSHIP *Gordon Wright*	3.00
_____COMPLETE TRAINING OF HORSE AND RIDER *Colonel Alois Podhajsky*	4.00
_____DISORDERS OF THE HORSE & WHAT TO DO ABOUT THEM *E. Hanauer*	2.00
_____DOG TRAINING MADE EASY & FUN *John W. Kellogg*	2.00
_____DRESSAGE—A Study of the Finer Points in Riding *Henry Wynmalen*	4.00
_____DRIVING HORSES *Sallie Walrond*	2.00
_____ENDURANCE RIDING *Ann Hyland*	2.00
_____EQUITATION *Jean Froissard*	4.00
_____FIRST AID FOR HORSES *Dr. Charles H. Denning, Jr.*	2.00
_____FUN OF RAISING A COLT *Rubye & Frank Griffith*	2.00
_____FUN ON HORSEBACK *Margaret Cabell Self*	4.00
_____GYMKHANA GAMES *Natlee Kenoyer*	2.00
_____HORSE DISEASES—Causes, Symptoms & Treatment *Dr. H. G. Belschner*	3.00
_____HORSE OWNER'S CONCISE GUIDE *Elsie V. Hanauer*	2.00
_____HORSE SELECTION & CARE FOR BEGINNERS *George H. Conn*	3.00
_____HORSE SENSE—A complete guide to riding and care *Alan Deacon*	4.00
_____HORSEBACK RIDING FOR BEGINNERS *Louis Taylor*	4.00
_____HORSEBACK RIDING MADE EASY & FUN *Sue Henderson Coen*	3.00
_____HORSES—Their Selection, Care & Handling *Margaret Cabell Self*	3.00
_____HOW TO BUY A BETTER HORSE & SELL THE HORSE YOU OWN	3.00
_____HOW TO ENJOY YOUR QUARTER HORSE *Williard H. Porter*	3.00
_____HUNTER IN PICTURES *Margaret Cabell Self*	2.00
_____ILLUSTRATED BOOK OF THE HORSE *S. Sidney* (8½″ x 11½″)	10.00
_____ILLUSTRATED HORSE MANAGEMENT—400 Illustrations *Dr. E. Mayhew*	5.00
_____ILLUSTRATED HORSE TRAINING *Captain M. H. Hayes*	5.00
_____ILLUSTRATED HORSEBACK RIDING FOR BEGINNERS *Jeanne Mellin*	2.00
_____JUMPING—Learning & Teaching *Jean Froissard*	3.00
_____KNOW ALL ABOUT HORSES *Harry Disston*	3.00
_____LAME HORSE—Causes, Symptoms & Treatment *Dr. James R. Rooney*	3.00
_____LAW & YOUR HORSE *Edward H. Greene*	3.00
_____LIPIZZANERS & THE SPANISH RIDING SCHOOL *W. Reuter* (4¼″ x 6″)	2.50
_____MANUAL OF HORSEMANSHIP *Harold Black*	5.00
_____MORGAN HORSE IN PICTURES *Margaret Cabell Self*	2.00
_____MOVIE HORSES—The Fascinating Techniques of Training *Anthony Amaral*	2.00
_____POLICE HORSES *Judith Campbell*	2.00
_____PRACTICAL GUIDE TO HORSESHOEING	2.00
_____PRACTICAL GUIDE TO OWNING YOUR OWN HORSE *Steven D. Price*	2.00
_____PRACTICAL HORSE PSYCHOLOGY *Moyra Williams*	3.00
_____PROBLEM HORSES Guide for Curing Serious Behavior Habits *Summerhays*	2.00
_____REINSMAN OF THE WEST—BRIDLES & BITS *Ed Connell*	4.00
_____RESCHOOLING THE THOROUGHBRED *Peggy Jett Pittenger*	3.00
_____RIDE WESTERN *Louis Taylor*	2.00
_____SCHOOLING YOUR YOUNG HORSE *George Wheatley*	2.00
_____STABLE MANAGEMENT FOR THE OWNER-GROOM *George Wheatley*	4.00
_____STALLION MANAGEMENT—A Guide for Stud Owners *A. C. Hardman*	3.00
_____TEACHING YOUR HORSE TO JUMP *W. J. Froud*	2.00
_____TRAIL HORSES & TRAIL RIDING *Anne & Perry Westbrook*	2.00
_____TRAINING YOUR HORSE TO SHOW *Neale Haley*	3.00
_____TREATING COMMON DISEASES OF YOUR HORSE *Dr. George H. Conn*	3.00
_____TREATING HORSE AILMENTS *G. W. Serth*	2.00
_____WESTERN HORSEBACK RIDING *Glen Balch*	2.00
_____WONDERFUL WORLD OF PONIES *Peggy Jett Pittenger* (8½″ x 11½″)	4.00
_____YOU AND YOUR PONY *Pepper Mainwaring Healey* (8½″ x 11″)	6.00
_____YOUR FIRST HORSE *George C. Saunders, M.D.*	3.00
_____YOUR PONY BOOK *Hermann Wiederhold*	2.00
_____YOUR WESTERN HORSE *Nelson C. Nye*	2.00

The books listed above can be obtained from your book dealer or directly from
Melvin Powers. When ordering, please remit 25c per book postage & handling.
Send for our free illustrated catalog of self-improvement books.

Melvin Powers
12015 Sherman Road, No. Hollywood, California 91605

NOTES